Everything A-Z Coloring and Learning Fun

by
Deepak Gupta

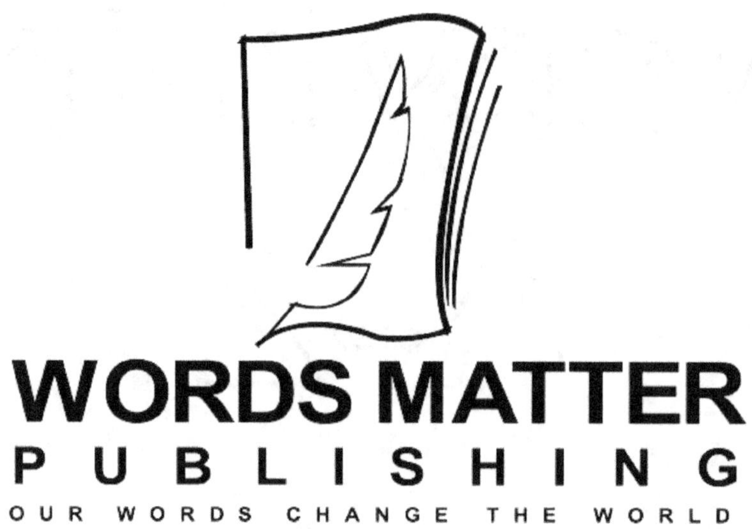

Words Matter Publishing
P.O. Box 531
Salem, Il 62881
www.wordsmatterpublishing.com

ISBN 13: 978-1-953912-21-3

Library of Congress Catalog Card Number: 2021941229

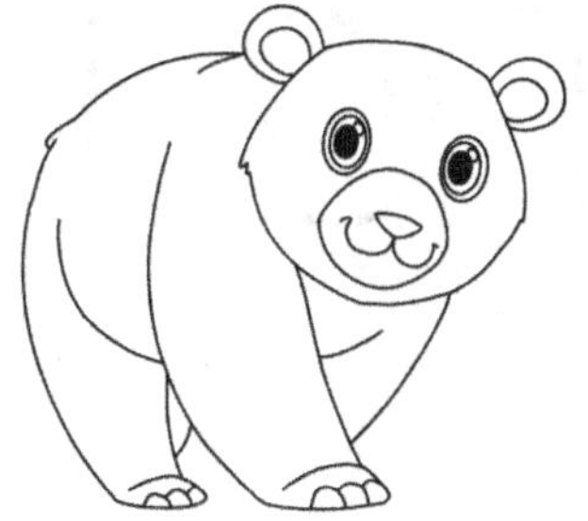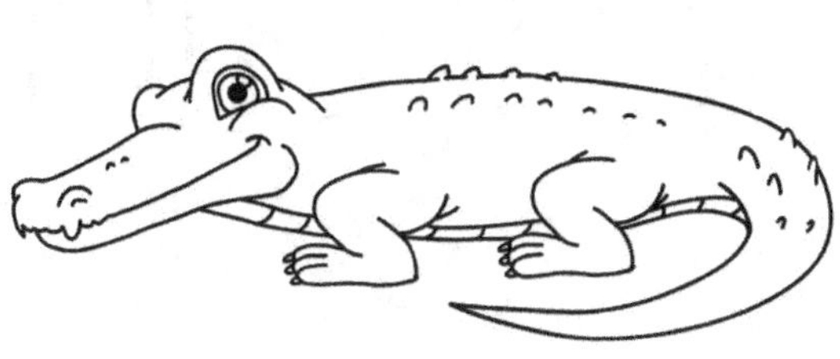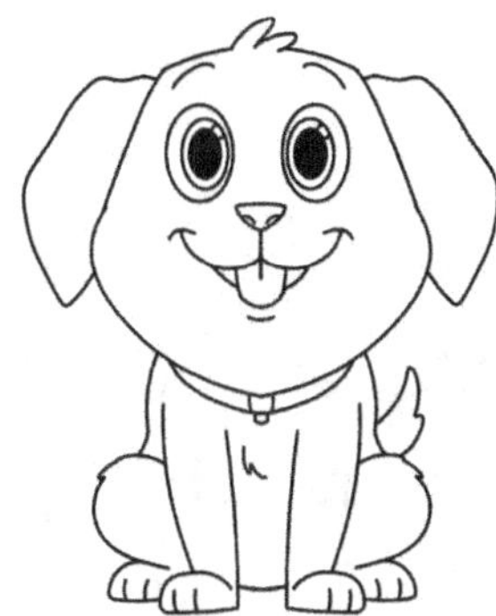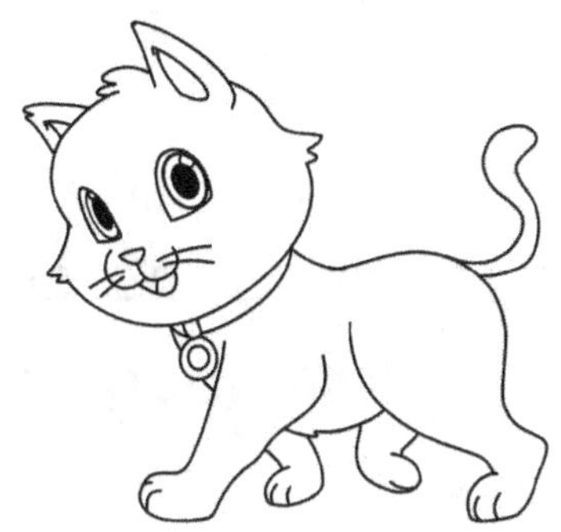

ANIMALS

Alligator

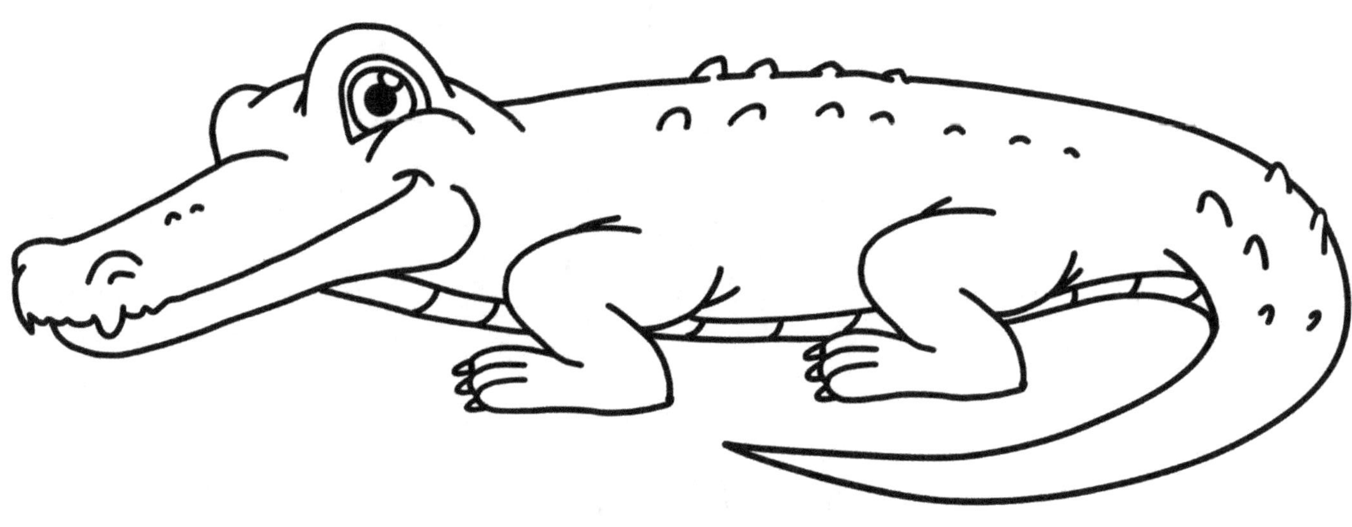

Alligator is a massive reptile with a long tail and short legs. It has tough skin, a broad snout and sharp teeth.

Bear

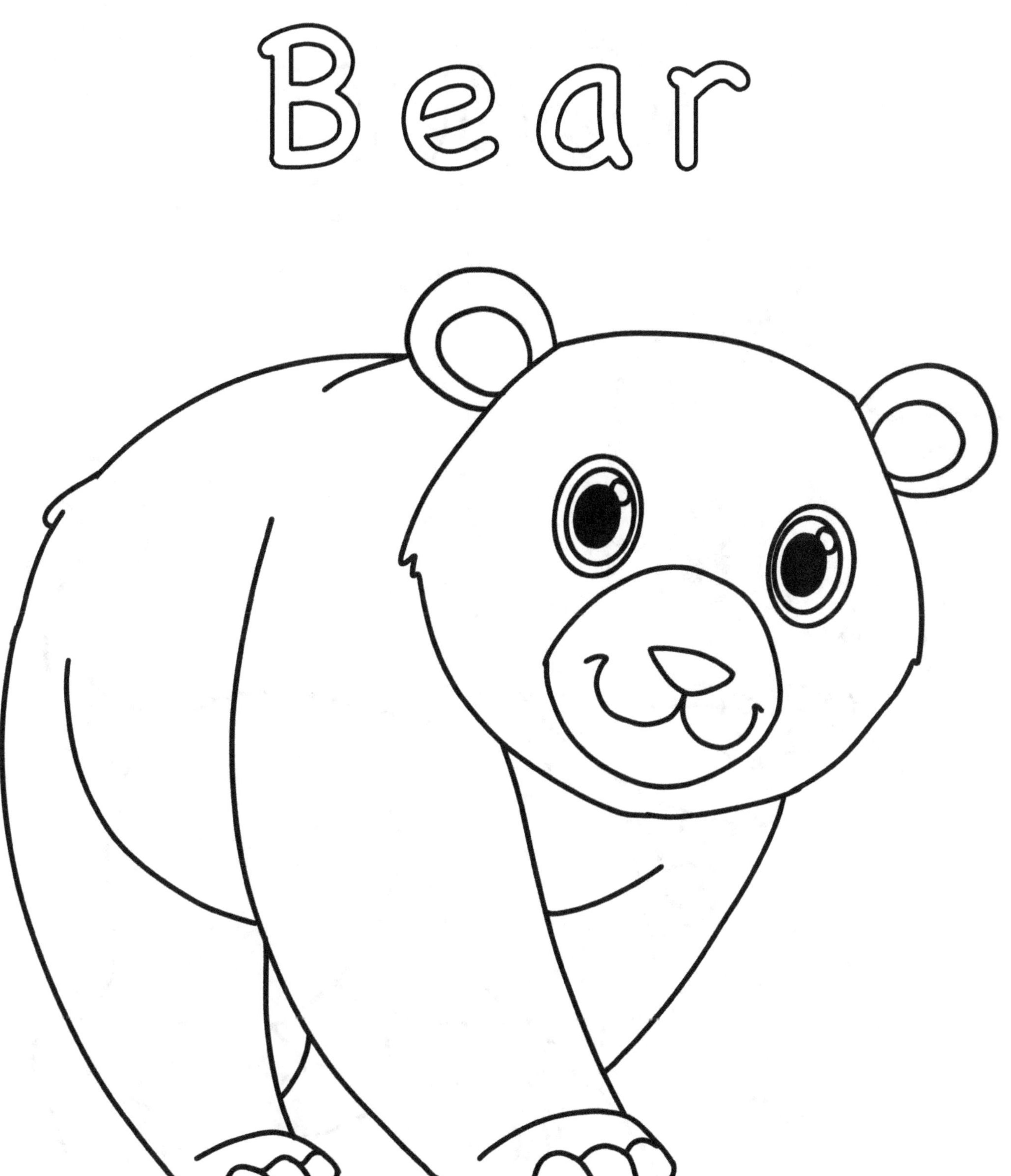

Bears are huge and heavy animals. But they can run very fast and can also climb trees easily.

Cat

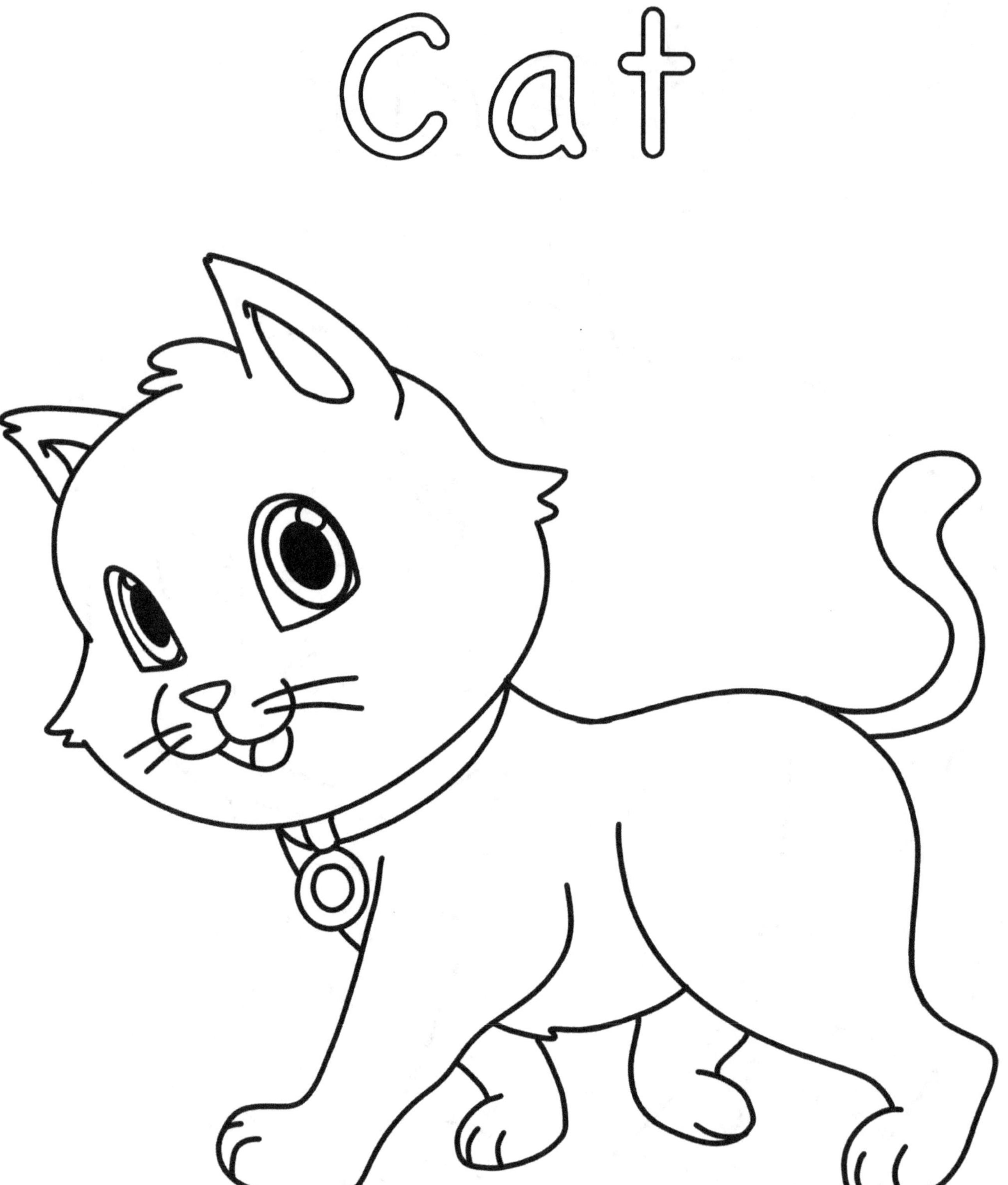

Cats are carnivorous animals with an excellent sense of vision
and hearing. They have sharp teeth and claws.
Cats can also be domestic.

Dog

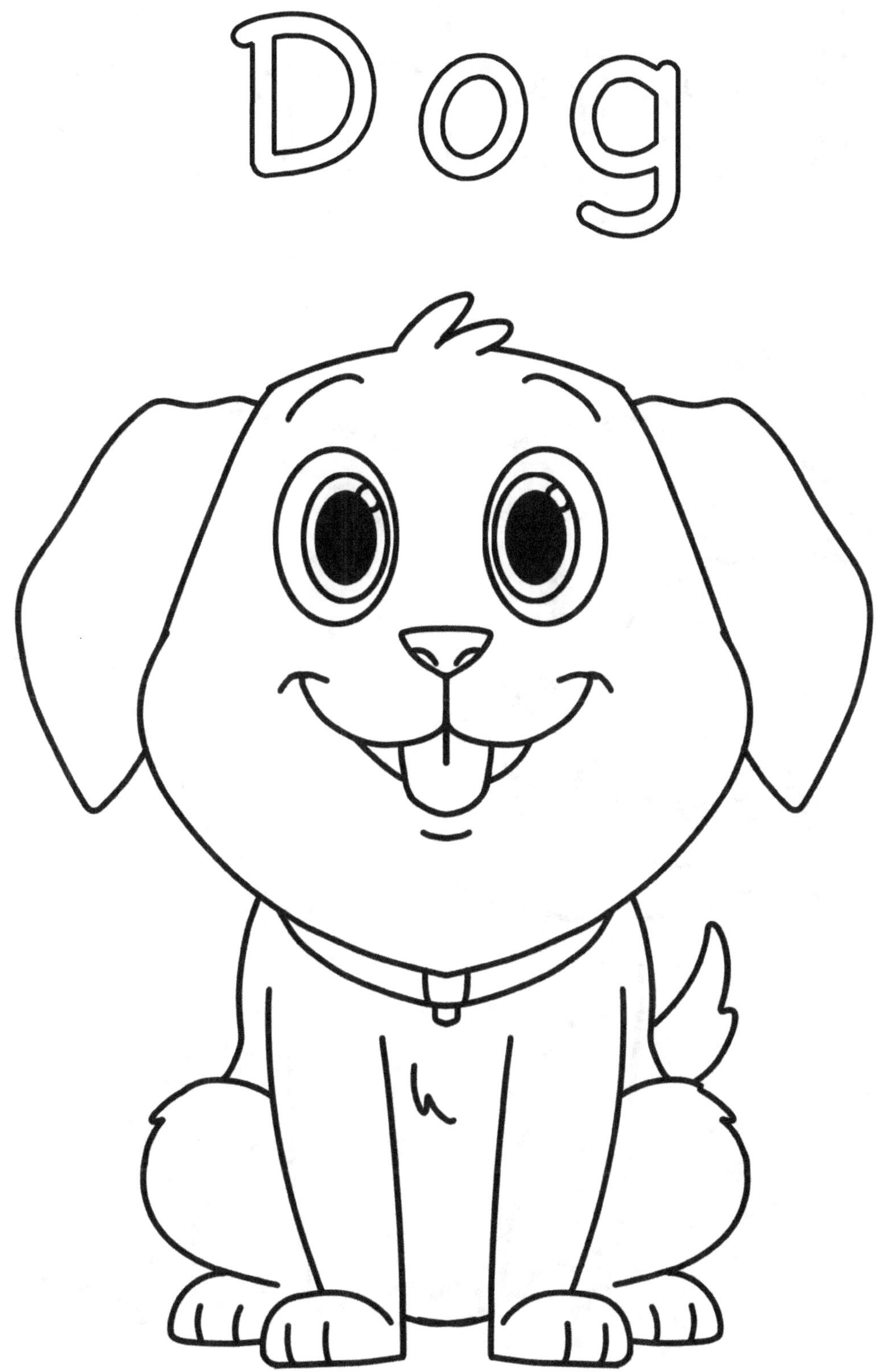

Dogs are pet animals and a human's best friend. They are very loyal to humans. Dogs are used in Army and Police to find objects that are hard to detect with a strong-smelling power.

Elephant

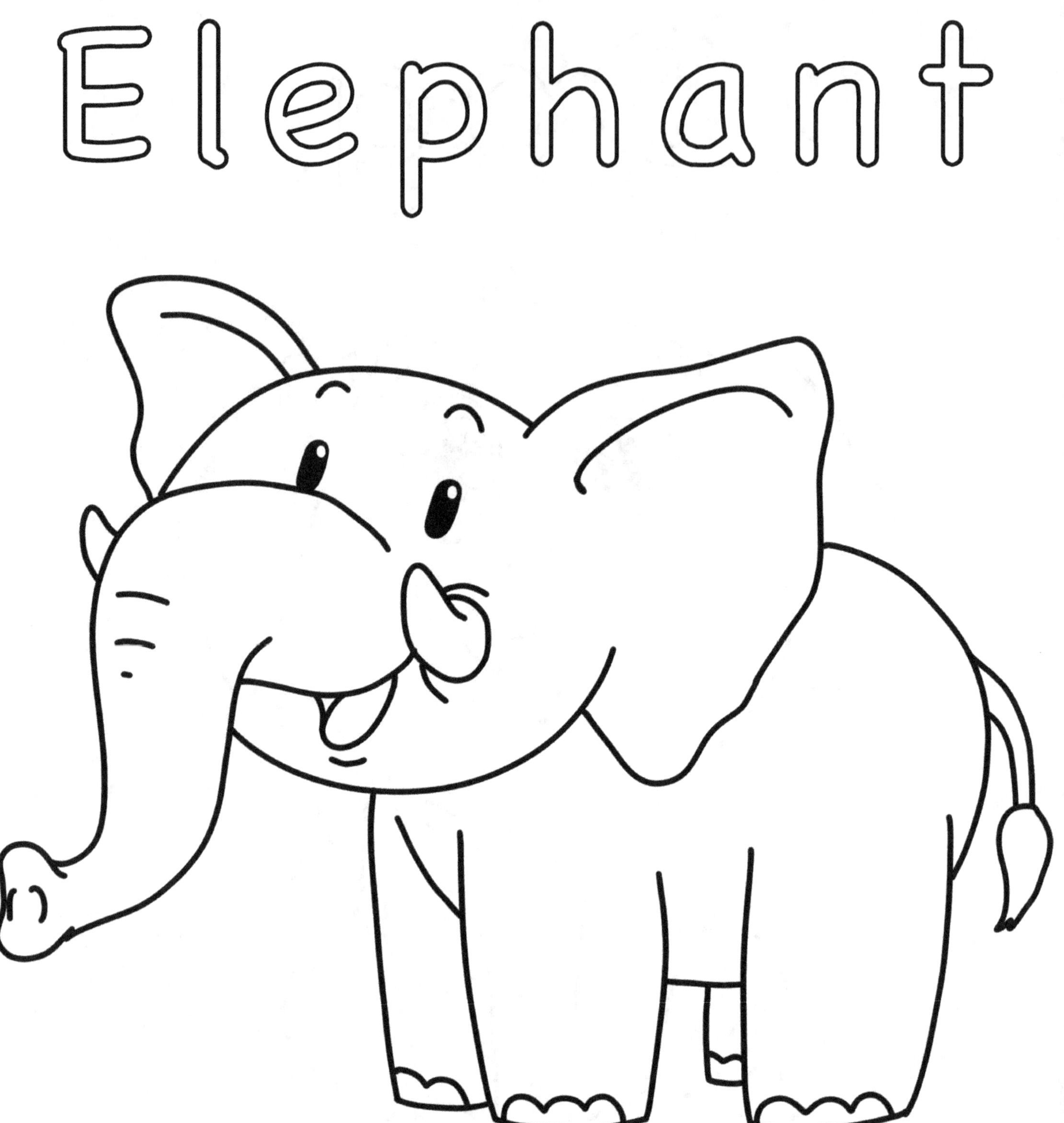

Elephants are huge mammals with large, thin ears. They have powerful trunks. Elephants use their tusks to dig water and eat fruits, vegetables, leaves, etc. Elephants are herbivores.

Fish

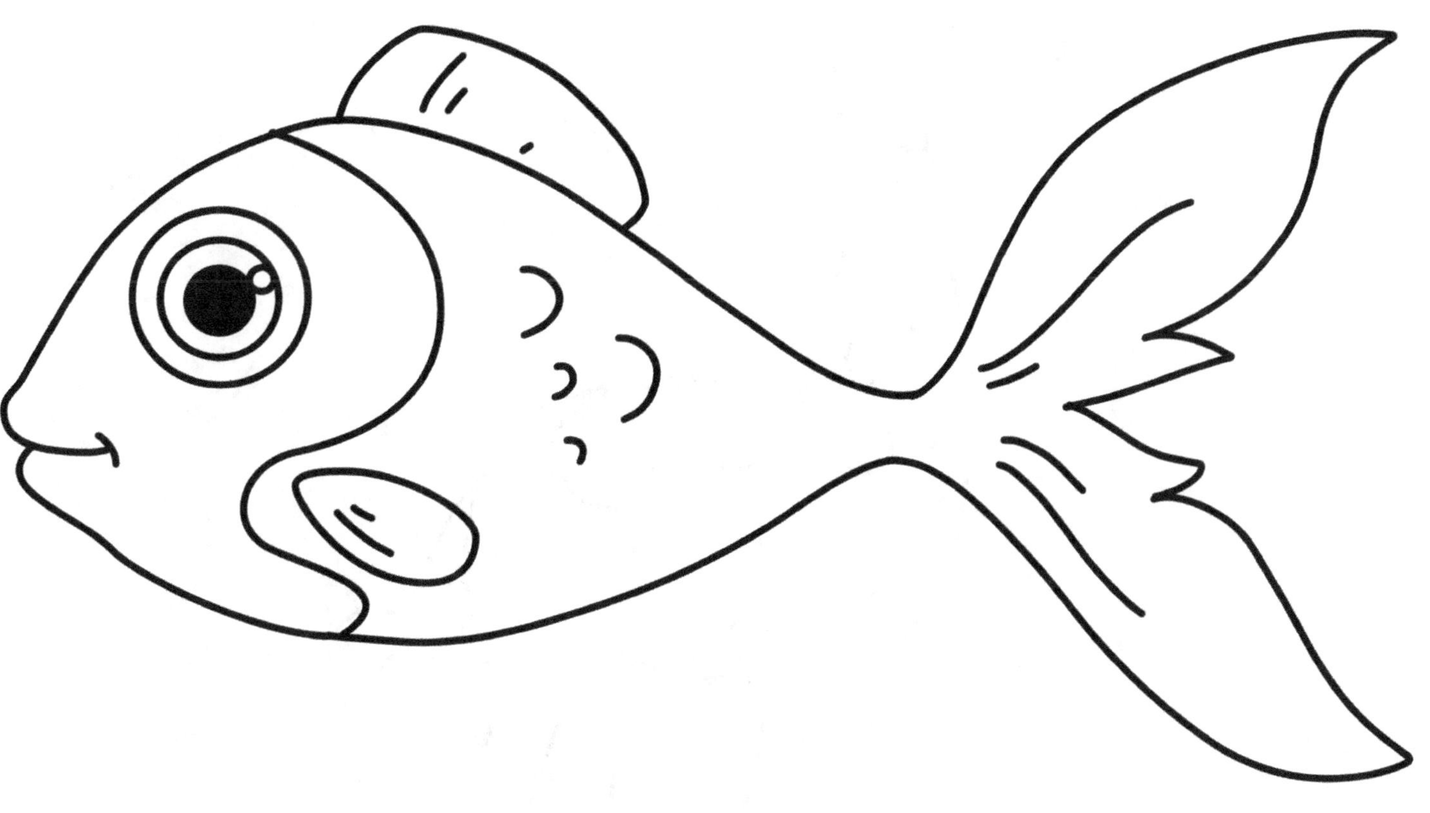

Fishes are aquatic animals. They live in water. Fishes have gills for breathing. Fishes have scales on their body with fins to swim.

Giraffe

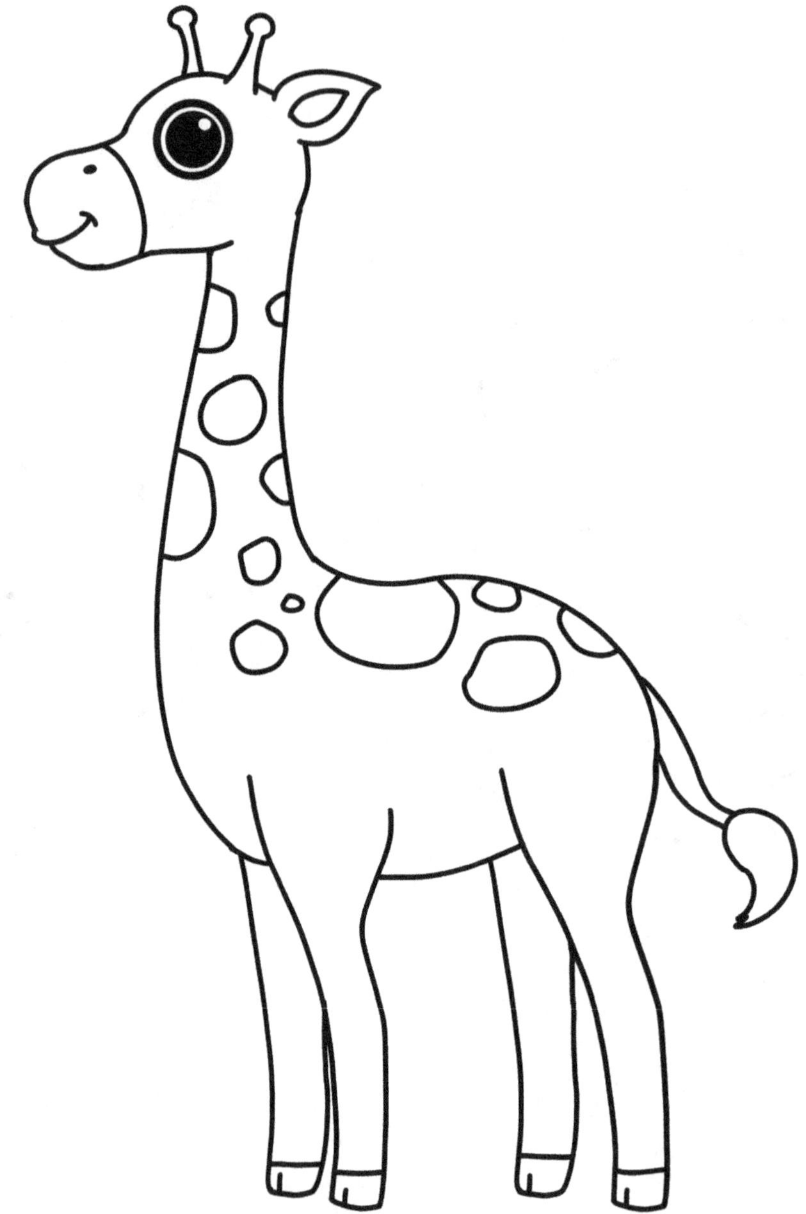

Giraffes are animals with a very long neck. They also have long legs and spots on their body.
Giraffes are herbivorous animals.

Horse

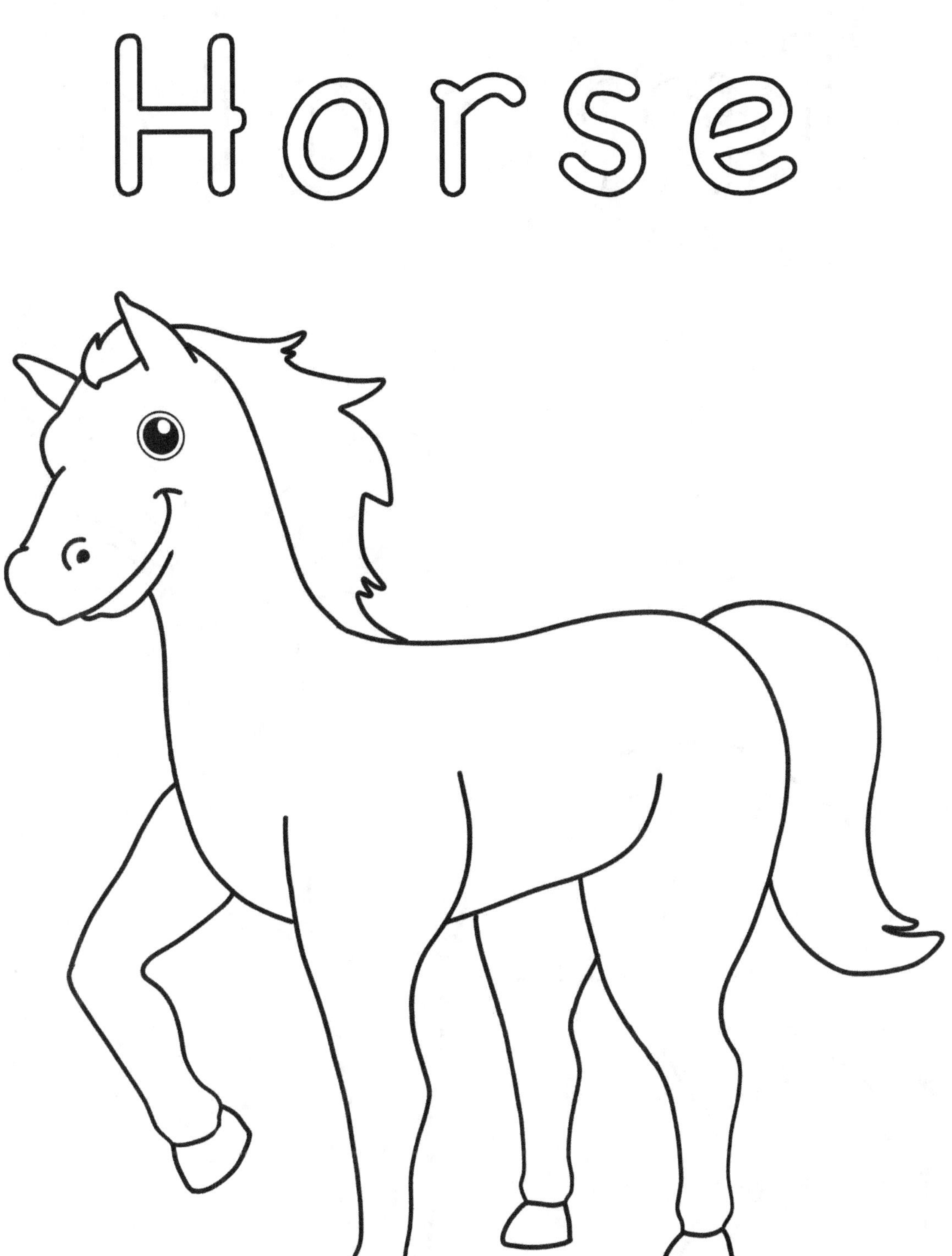

Horses are human-friendly animals.
These 4-legged animals have been a great help
for humans for a very long time.

Impala

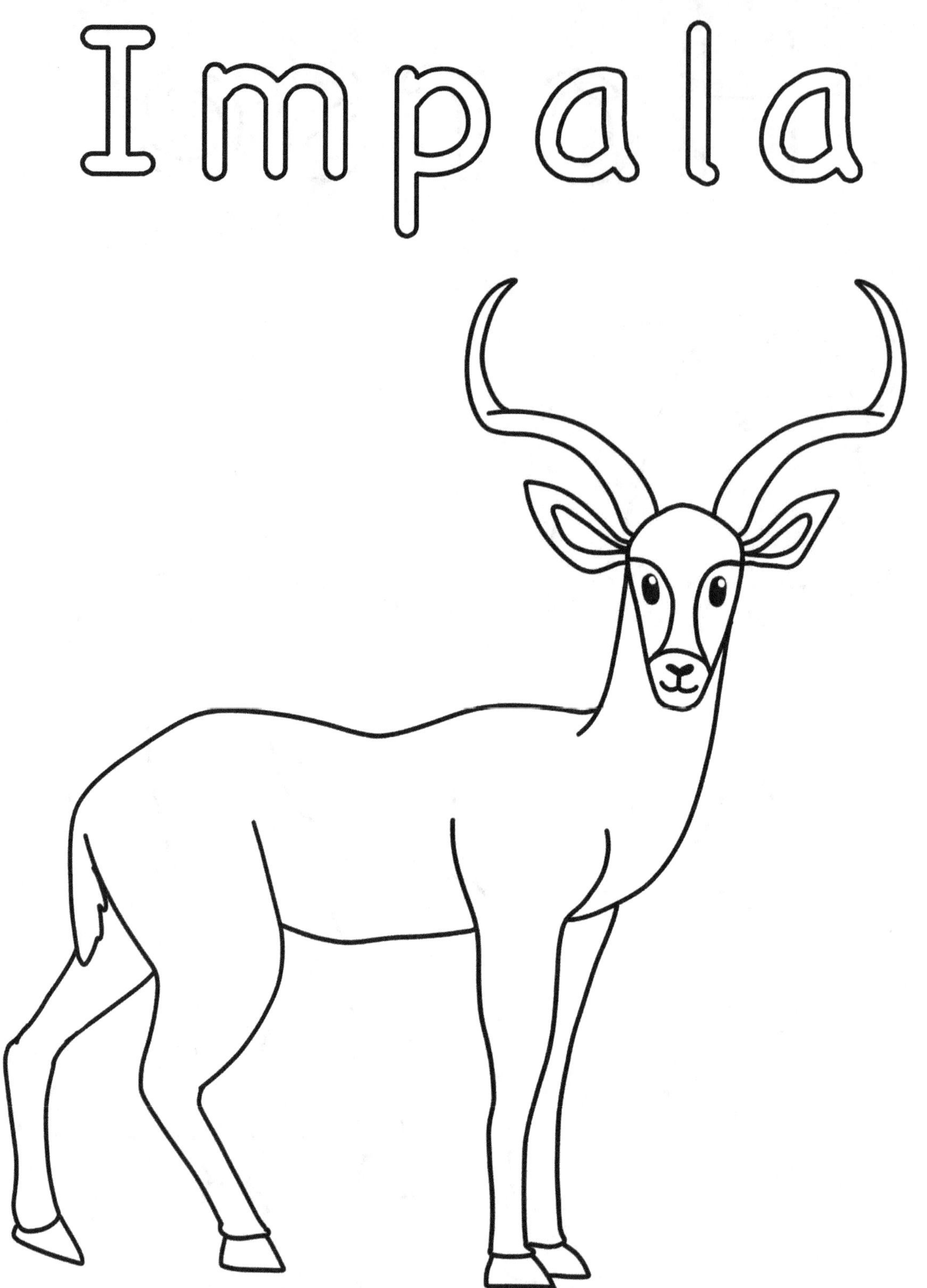

Impala is an antelope. It is mainly found in Southern Africa and Eastern Africa. They live in hot, dry grasslands, woodlands with few trees or in the savanna.

Jellyfish

Jellyfish are made up of a bag-like smooth body.
They have tentacles armed with stinging, tiny cells.
Jellyfish don't have a heart, bones, brain or eyes.

Kangaroo

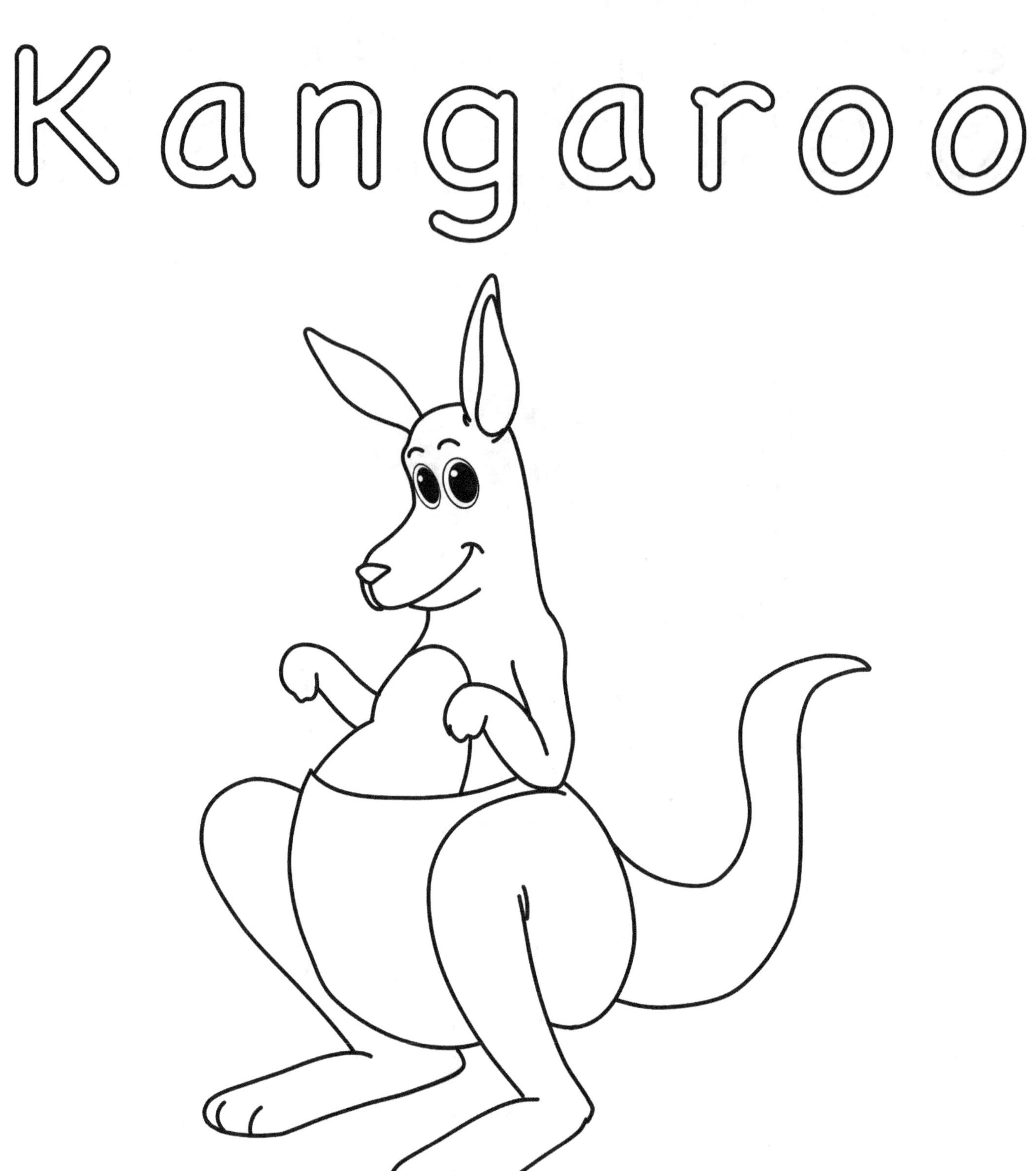

Kangaroos are animals with tiny front legs and strong, long tail.
Kangaroos use their tails for balance while jumping.
Kangaroos can jump very high.

Lion

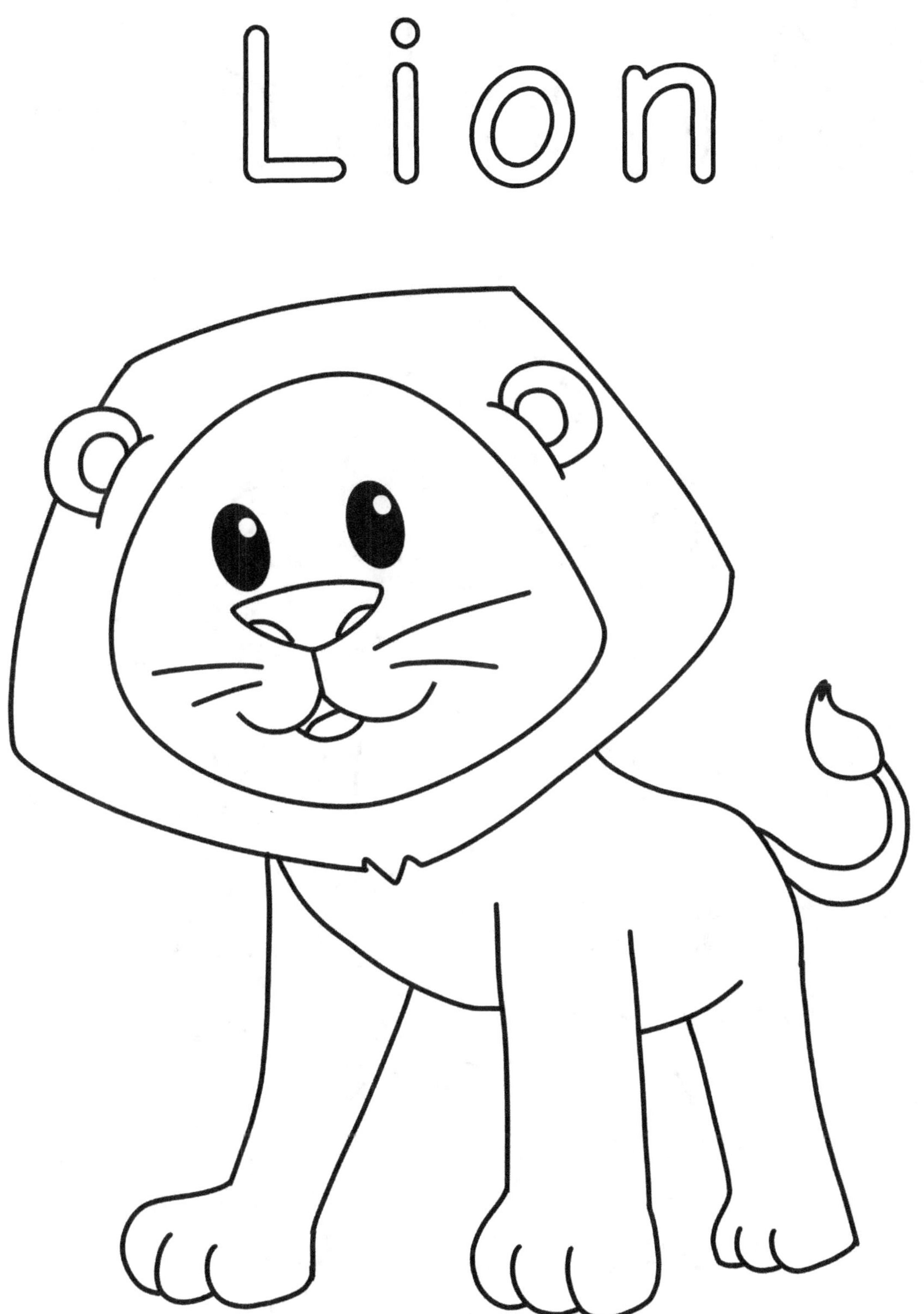

Famously called the "King of the jungle", a lion is a carnivorous animal. They have compact, muscular bodies. Female lions are the primary hunters.

Monkey

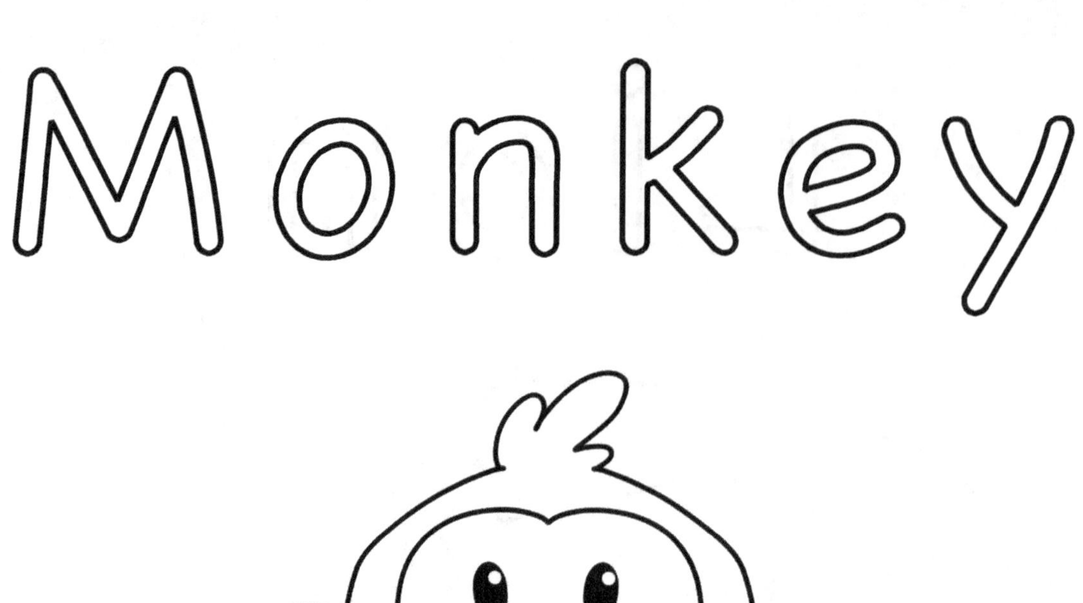

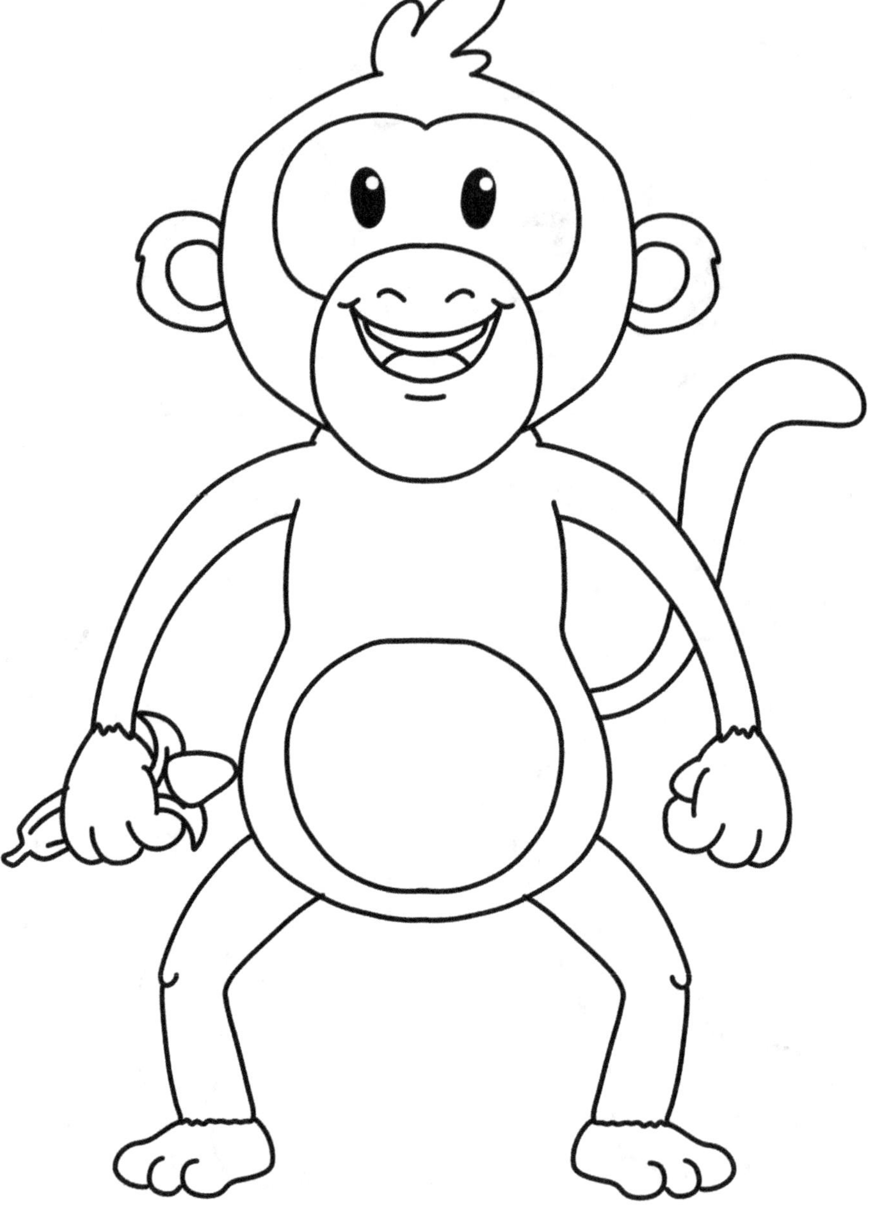

Monkeys are clever and social animals. They can run and leap on trees with ease. Monkeys are also primates, just like humans.

Narwhal

Narwhal looks like a hybrid of a whale and a unicorn.
It has a long, spiralled tusk on its head.
Some males may even have two tusks.

Owl

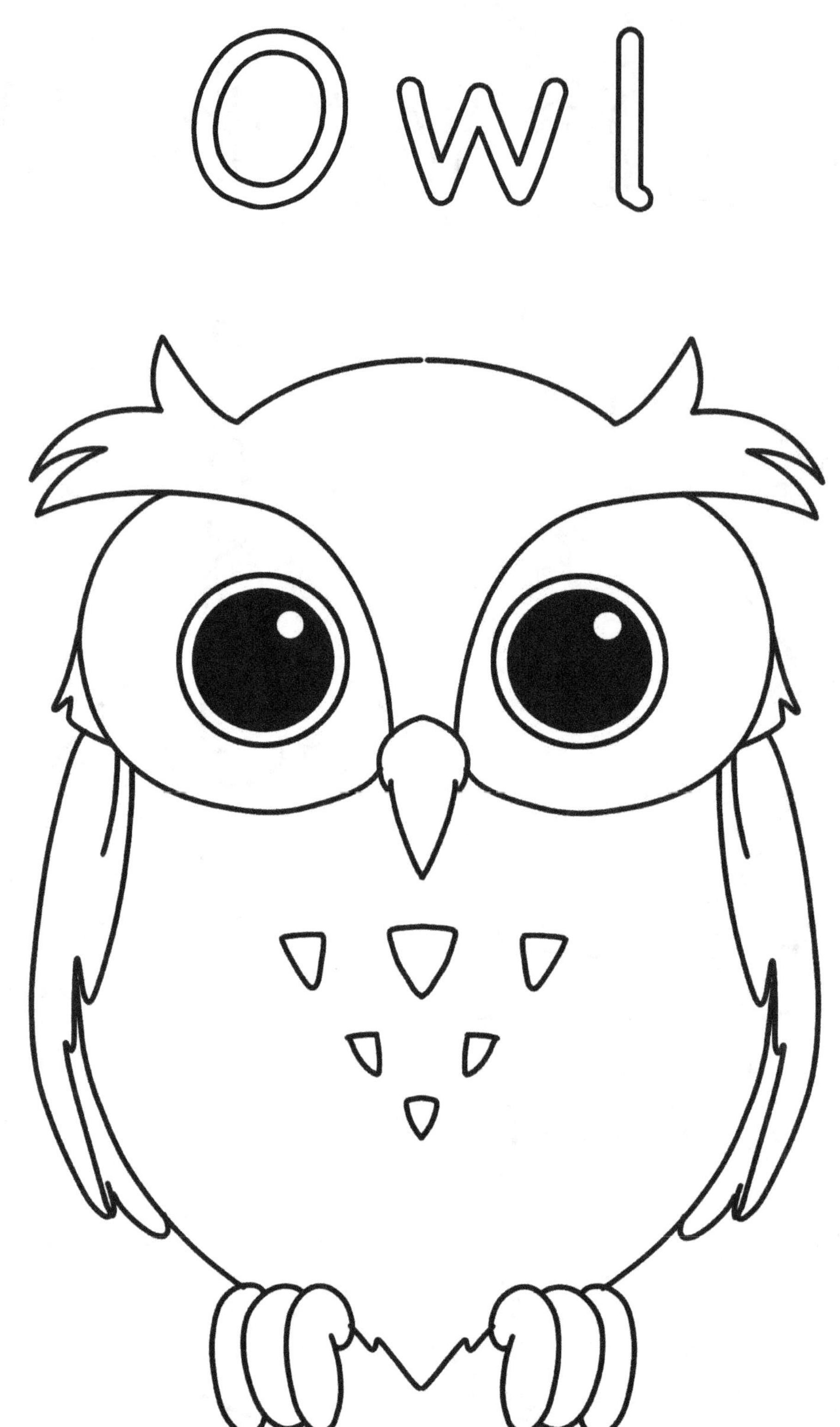

Owls are nocturnal animals.
They sleep during the day and stay awake at night.
They hunt for food at night.

Panther

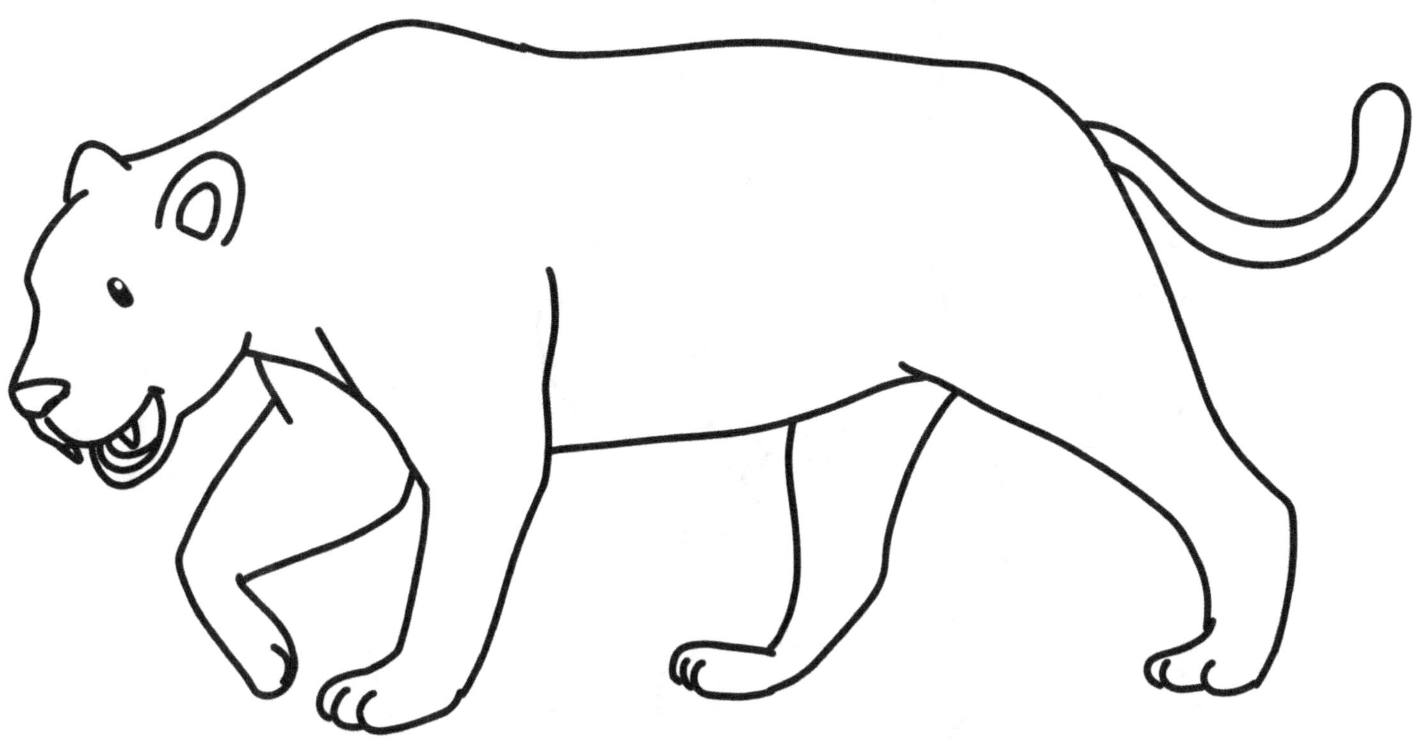

"Ghost of the forest" is another name for the Black Panther. Panthers are good at hiding and stalking their preys at night.

Quokka

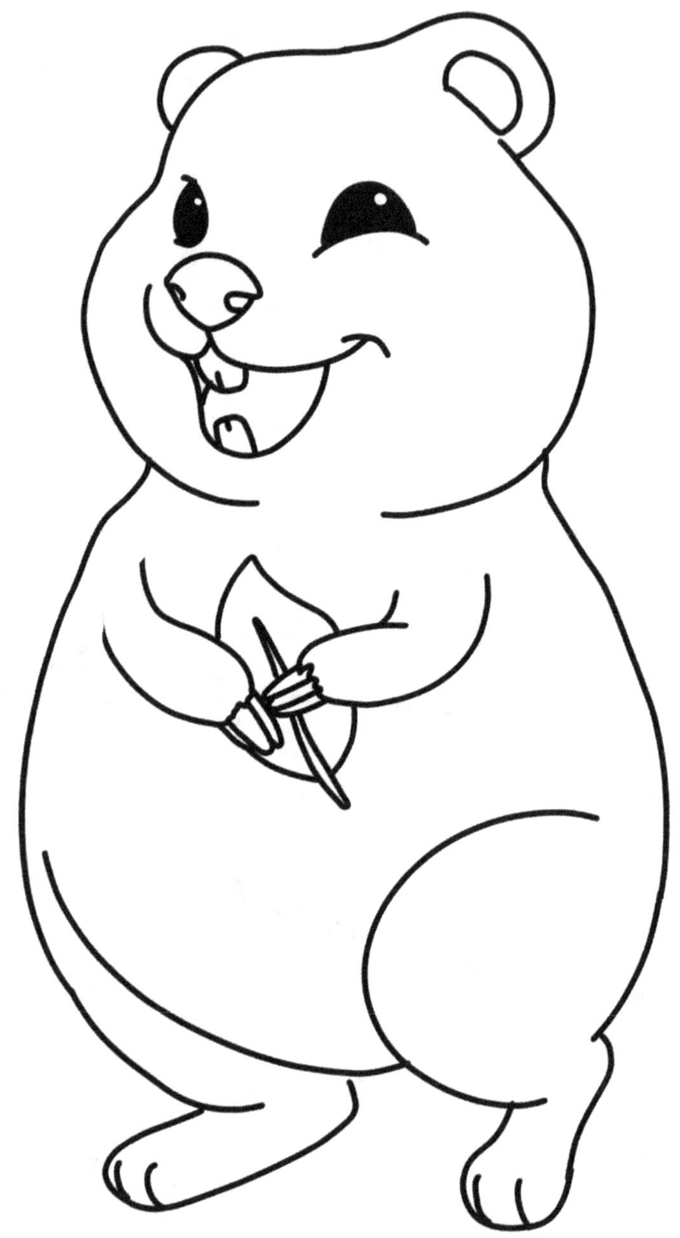

Quokka is a cute animal the size of a rabbit or a cat.
It has a long skinny tail.
People often mistake Quokka for a rat.

Rhino

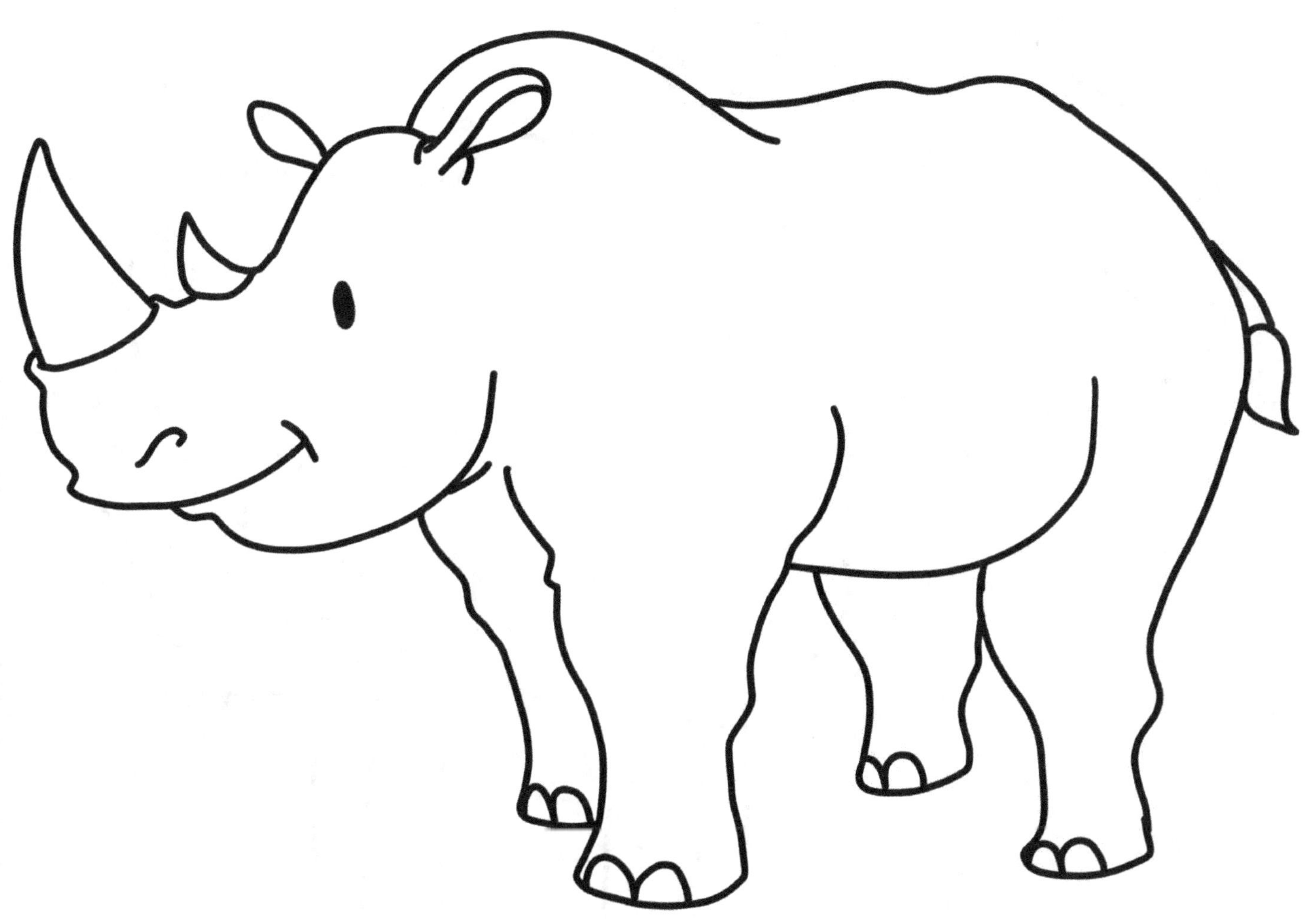

Rhinos are large animals with small brains.
They have a horn on their snout.
Rhinos are herbivorous mammals with poor vision.

Sheep

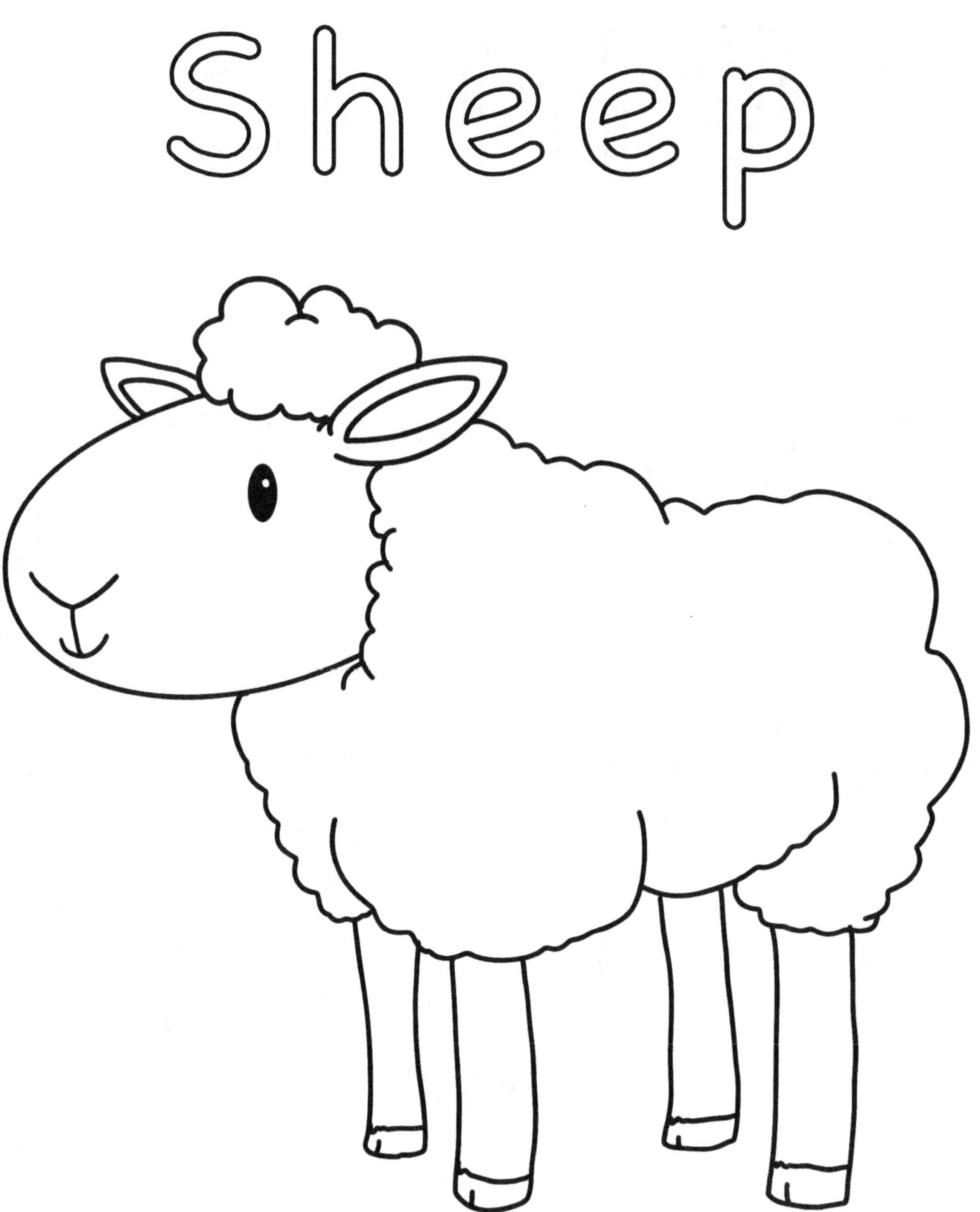

Sheep are domestic animals. Sheep are raised on farms.
They give us milk, meat and wool.
The name for a group of sheep is "flock".

Turtle

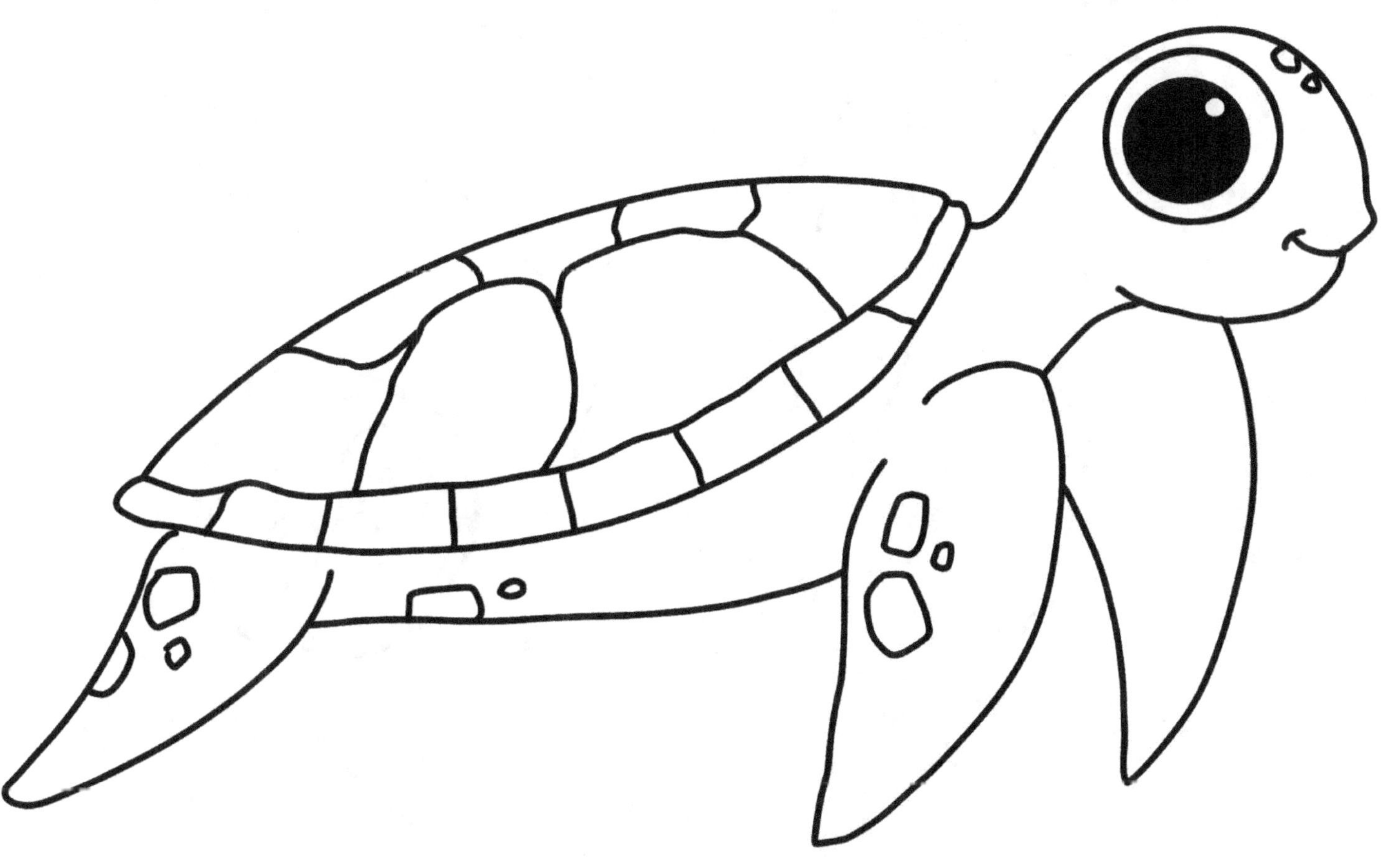

Turtles are shy animals. They cover themselves with their shell when in trouble. Turtles like to remain in the water for protection.

Unau

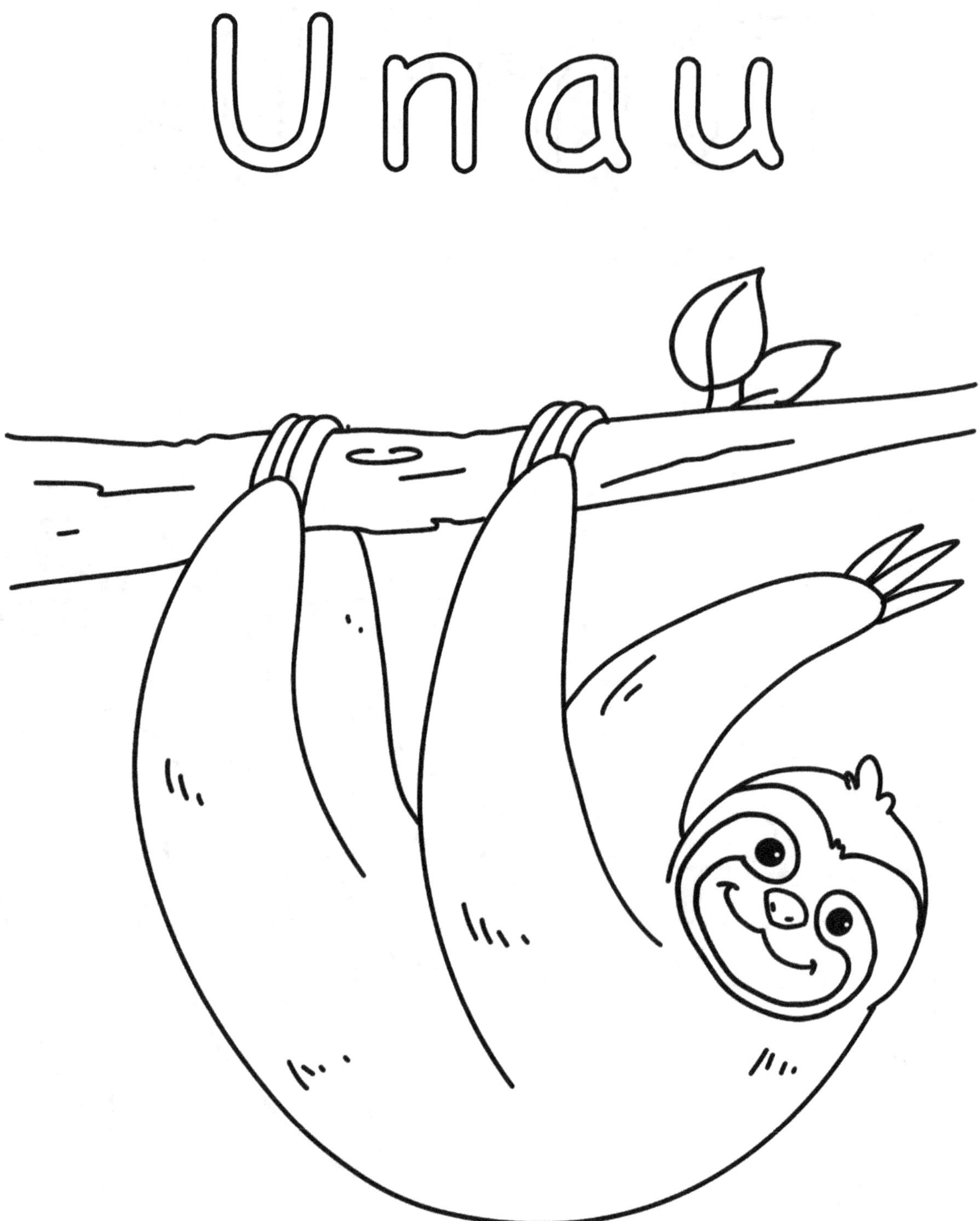

Sloths have long arms and shaggy fur.
They look like monkeys and live in tropical forests.
They are related to anteaters and armadillos.

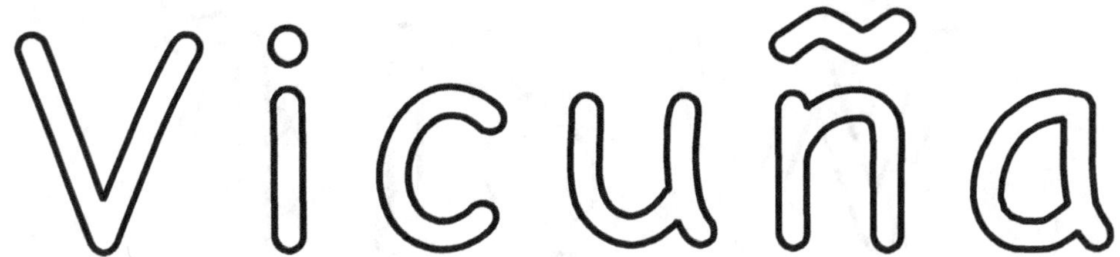

Vicuña

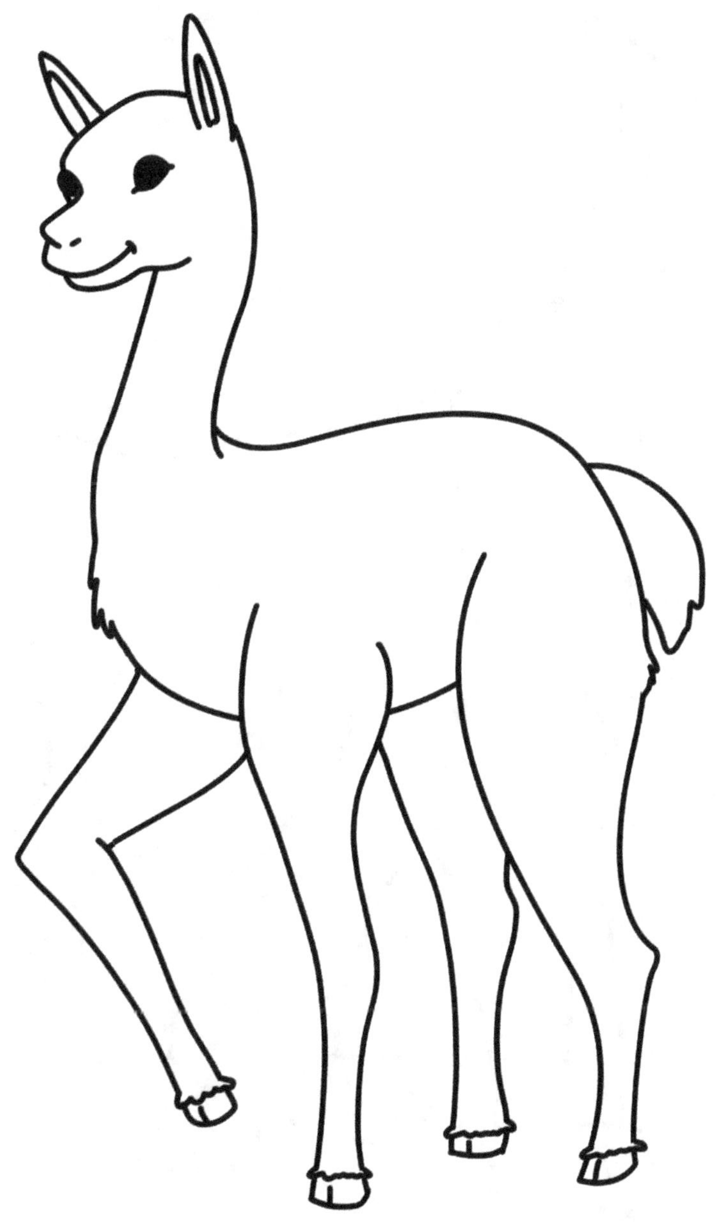

Vicunas are related to llama. Vicunas have soft hair. They belong to the camelid family. They have a small, wedge-shaped head with forward-facing eyes.

Wolf

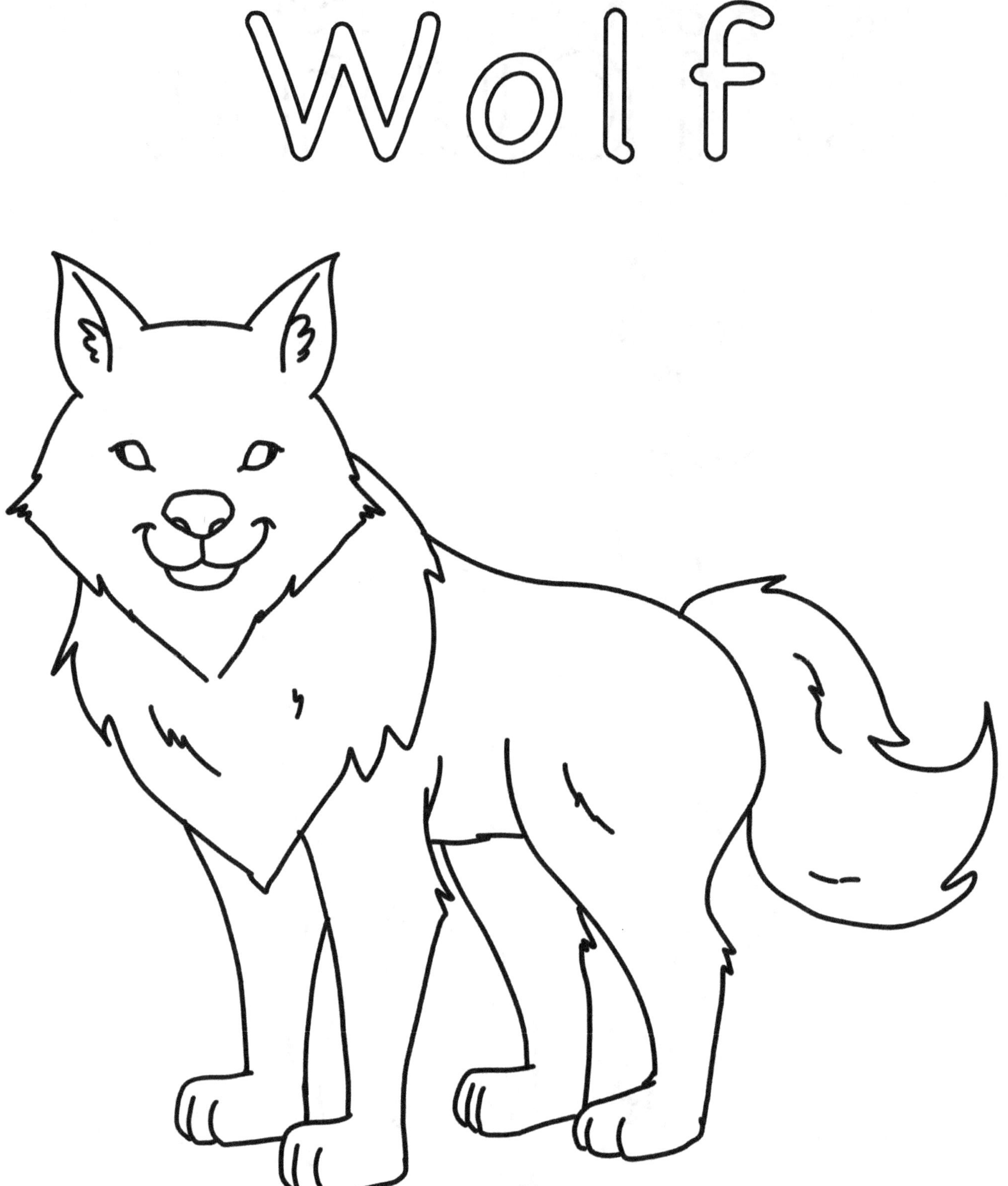

Wolves are mammals. They belong to the dog family.
A fully grown wolf can weigh 200 pounds.
Wolves live in groups called "packs".

Xray Fish

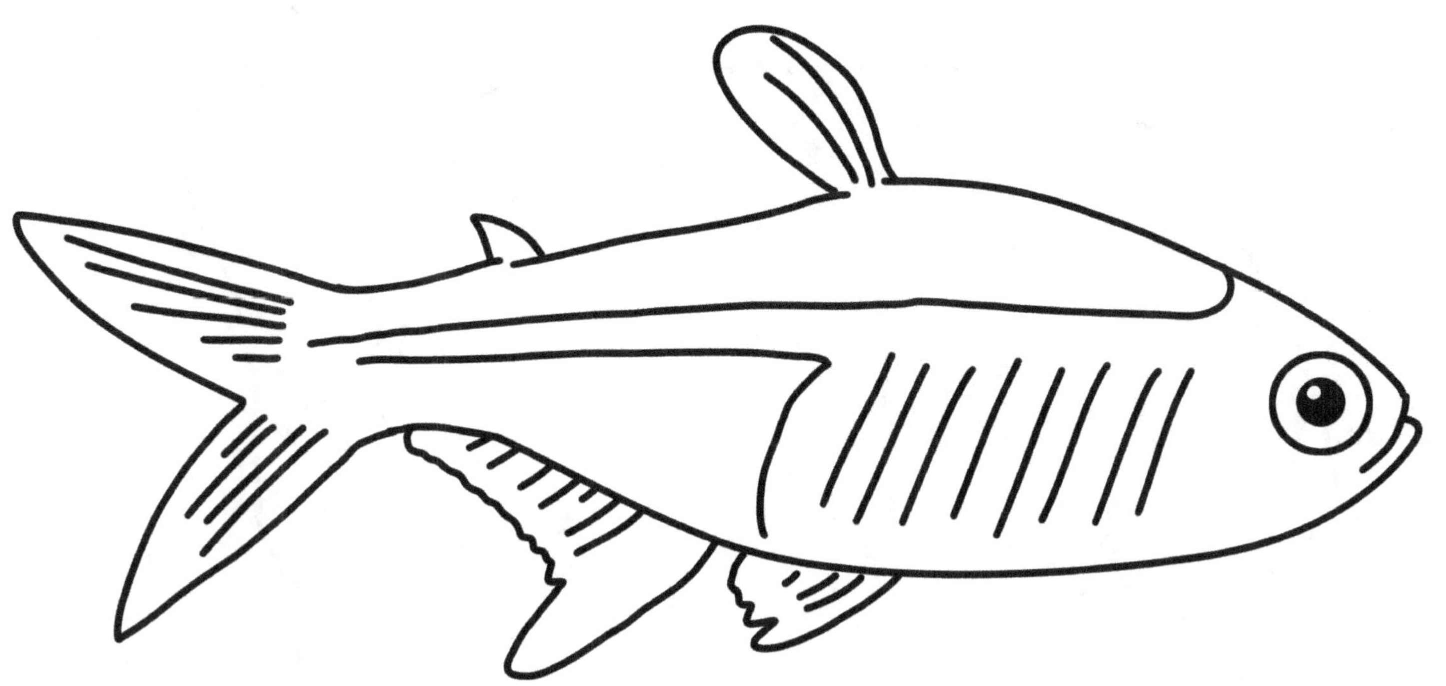

X-ray fishes got this name because of their translucent skin layer. The backbone of an x-ray fish is visible through its skin. It's a small fish.

Yak

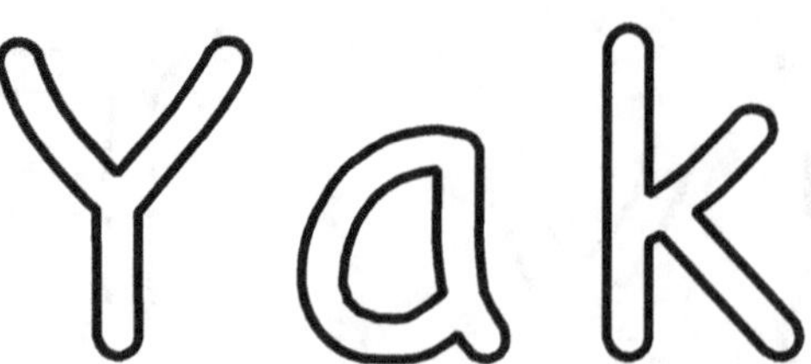

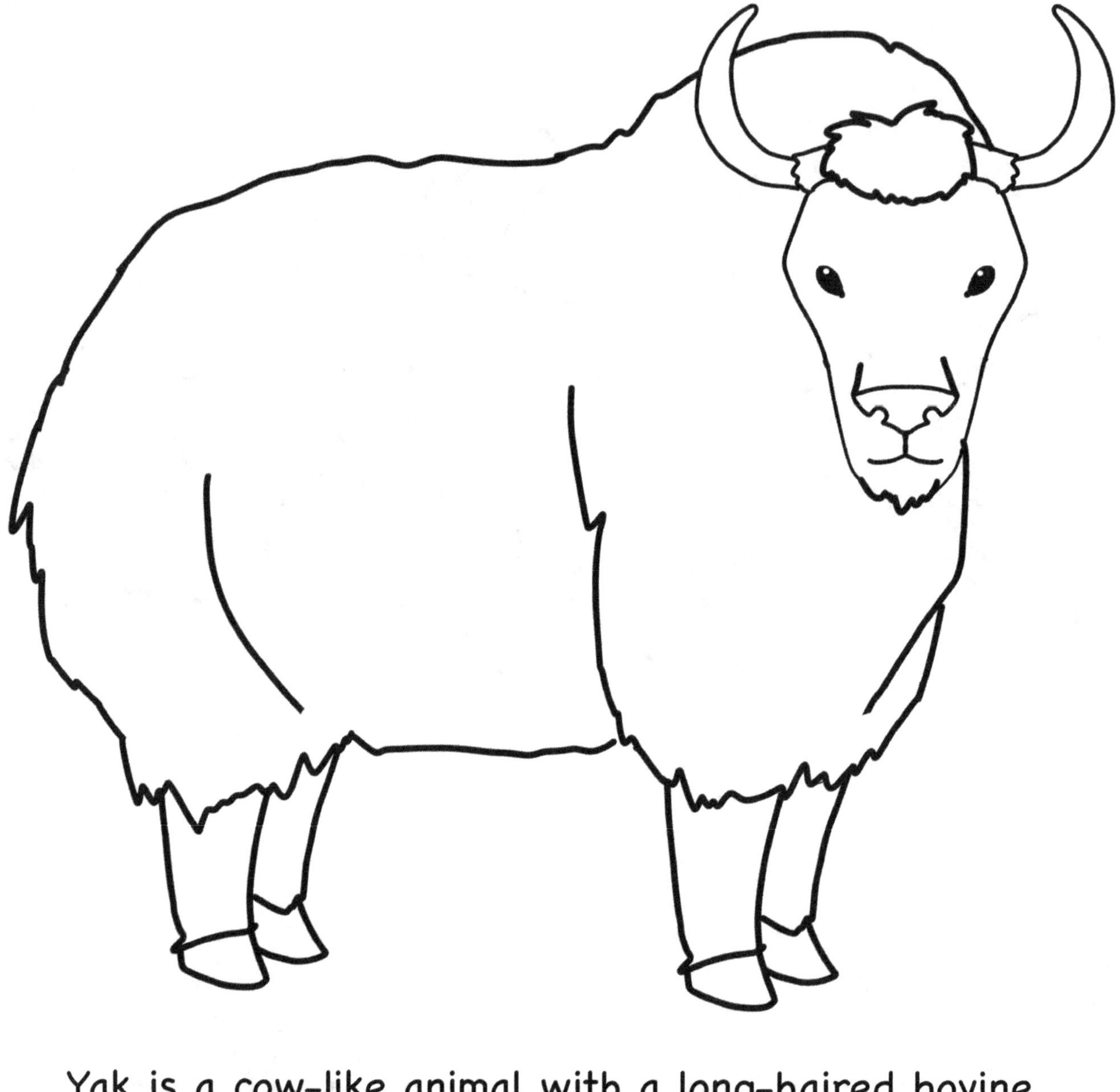

Yak is a cow-like animal with a long-haired bovine.
They live in the Himalayan region. Yaks have long, thick hair
that keeps them warm in cold climates.

Zebra

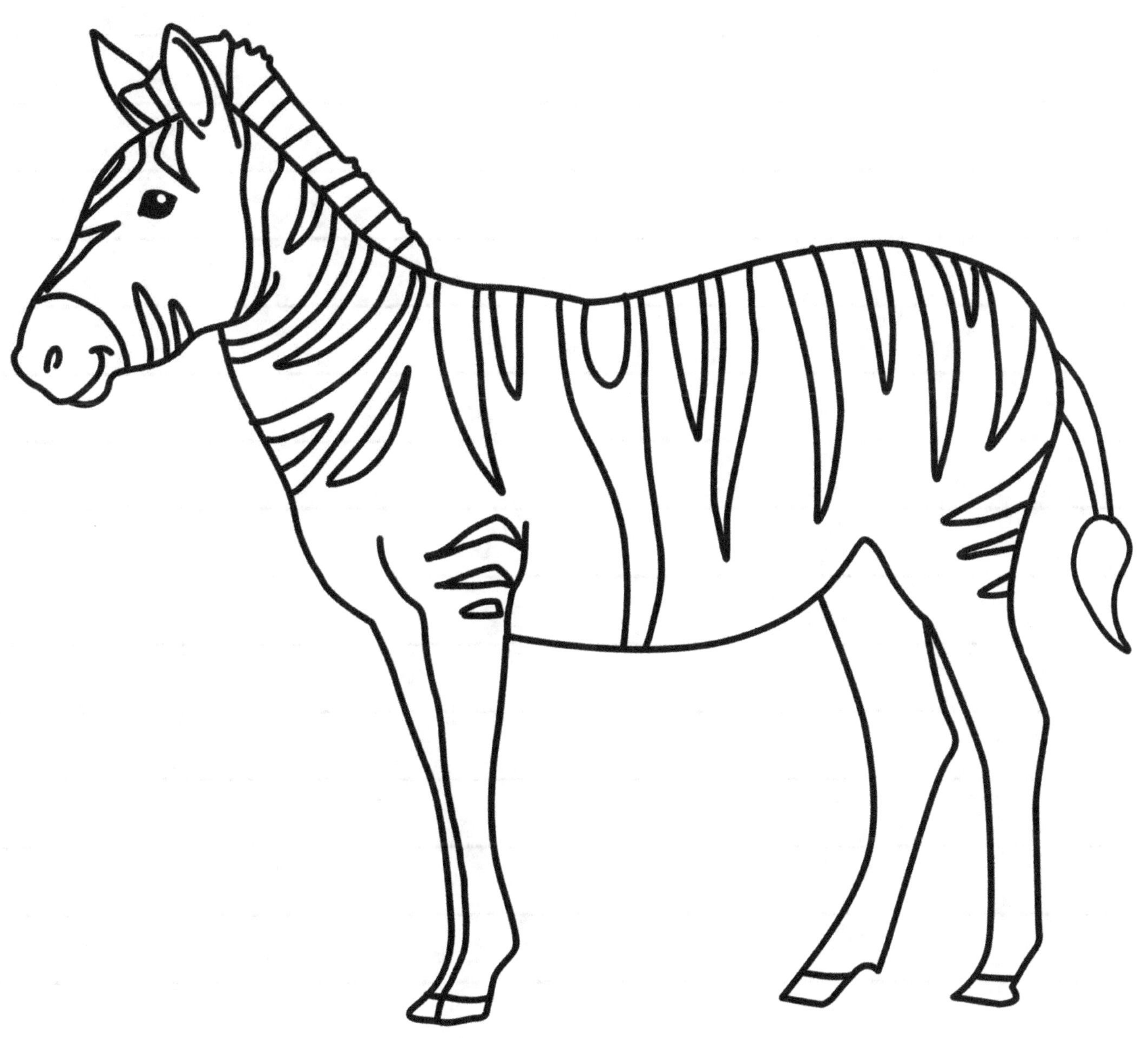

Zebras look like horses. There bodies are covered
with black and white stripes.
Zebras have excellent hearing and eyesight.

Name your favorite animal and write a few lines about it

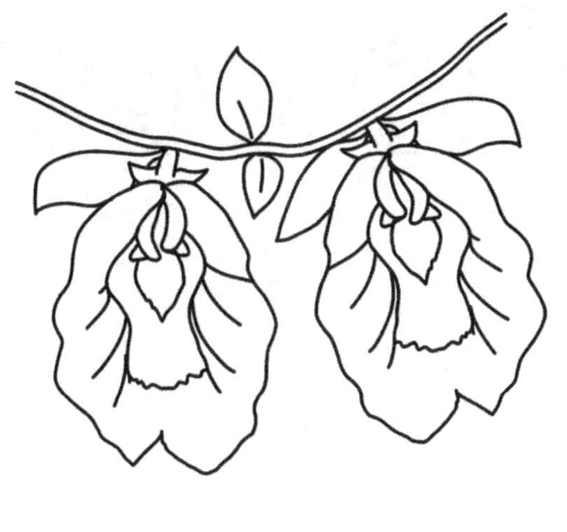
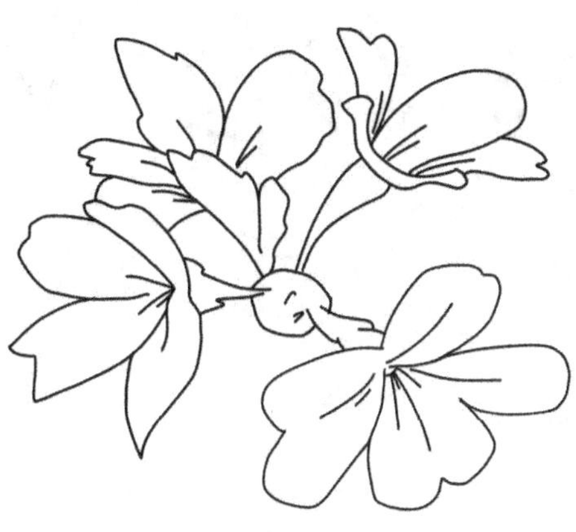

FLOWERS

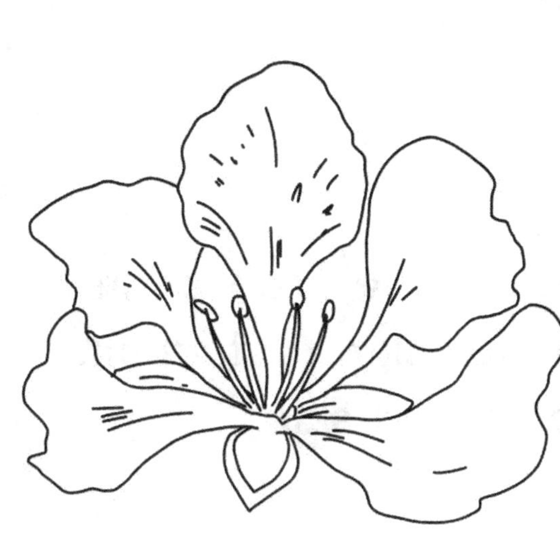
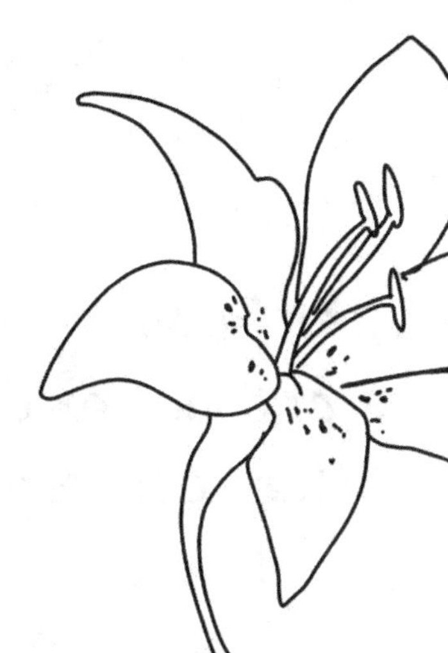

Aloe Vera Flower

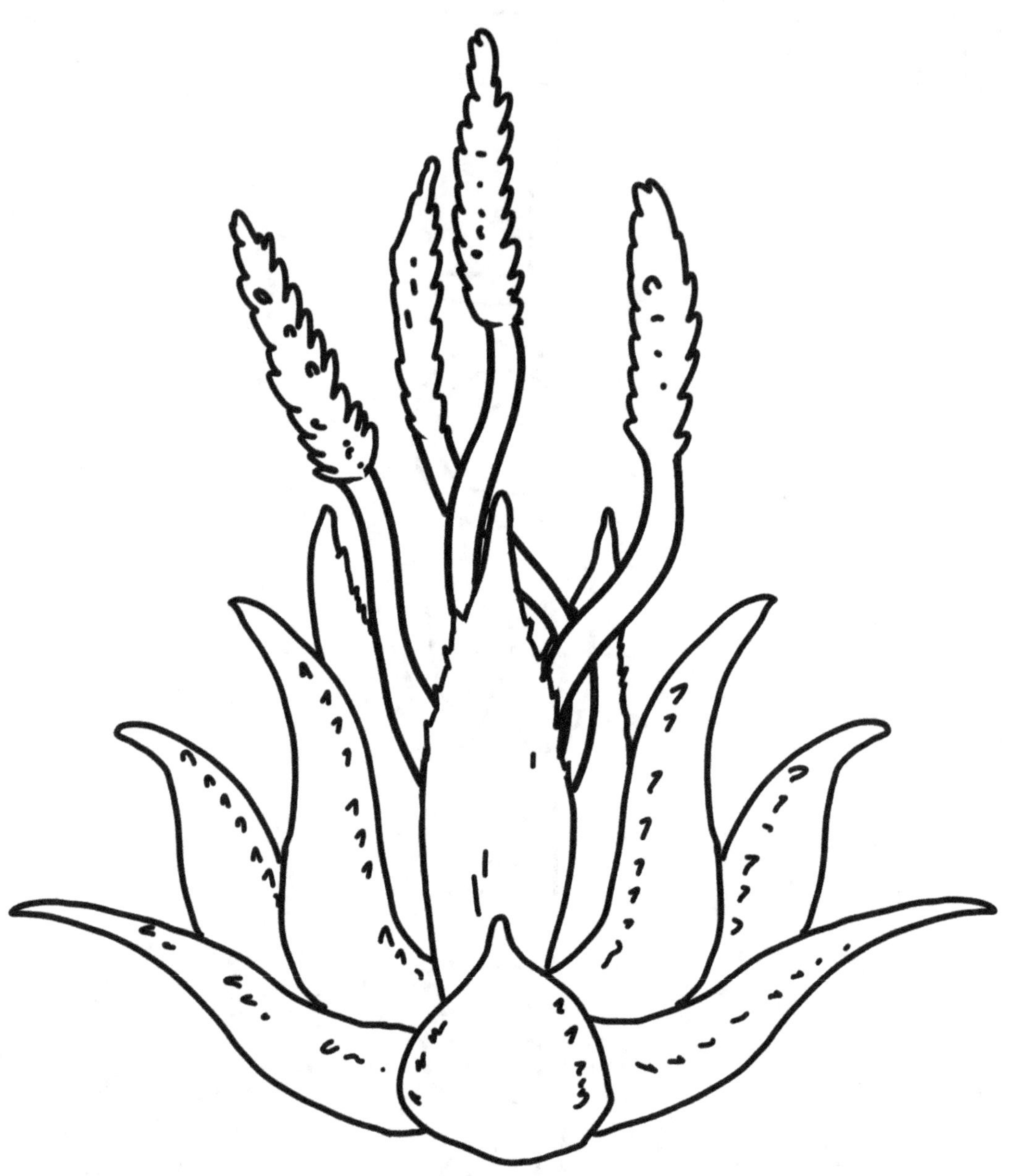

Aloe Vera flowers are pendulous leaves. These are rich in vitamins and antioxidants. People use it for skin protection. They can repair your UV-ray damaged skin.

Butterfly Pea

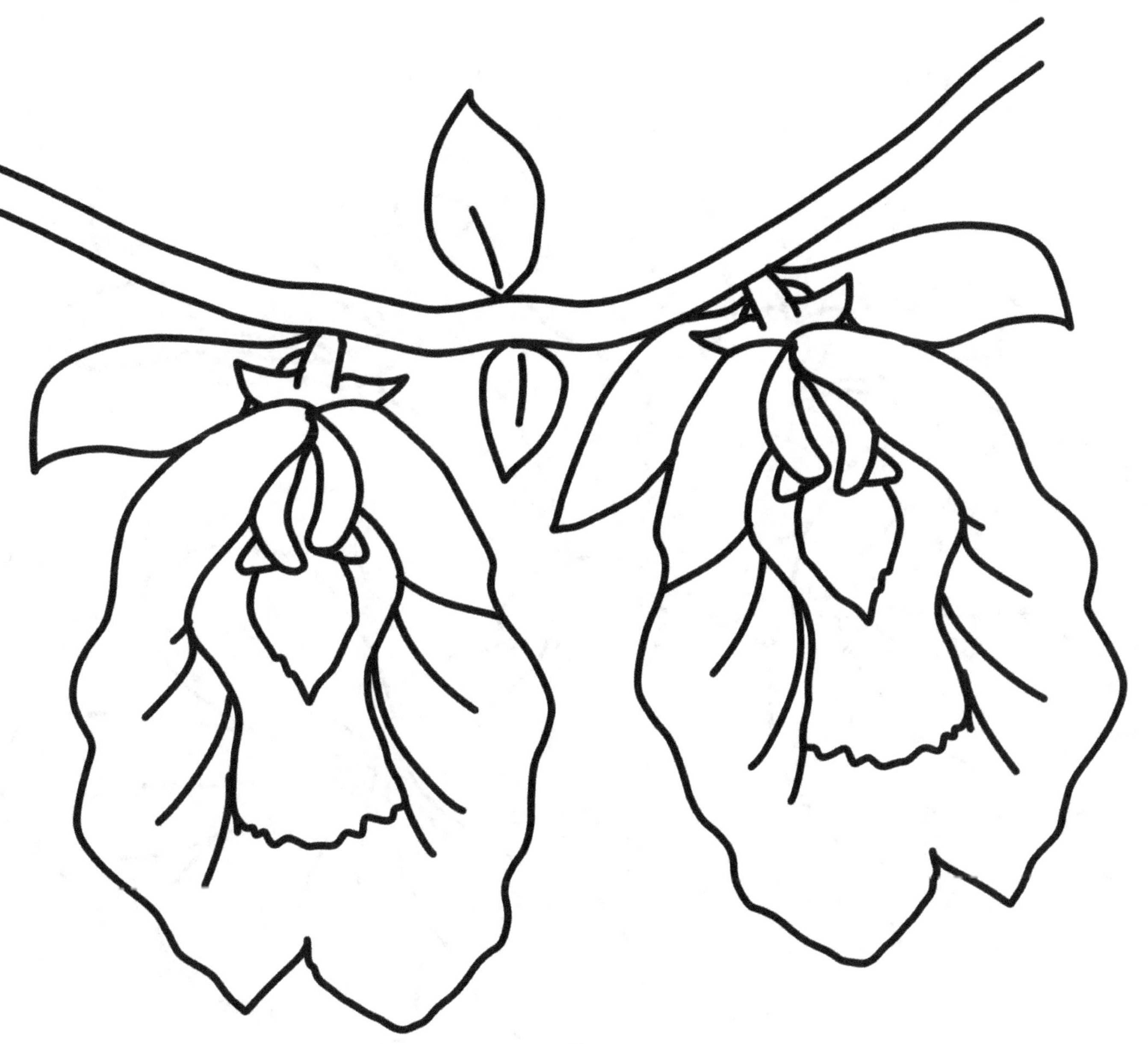

Butterfly pea is a perennial vine that can grow up to 3 feet long. It is not a climbing vine but a twinning vine. Hence, it extends along the ground.

Crossandra

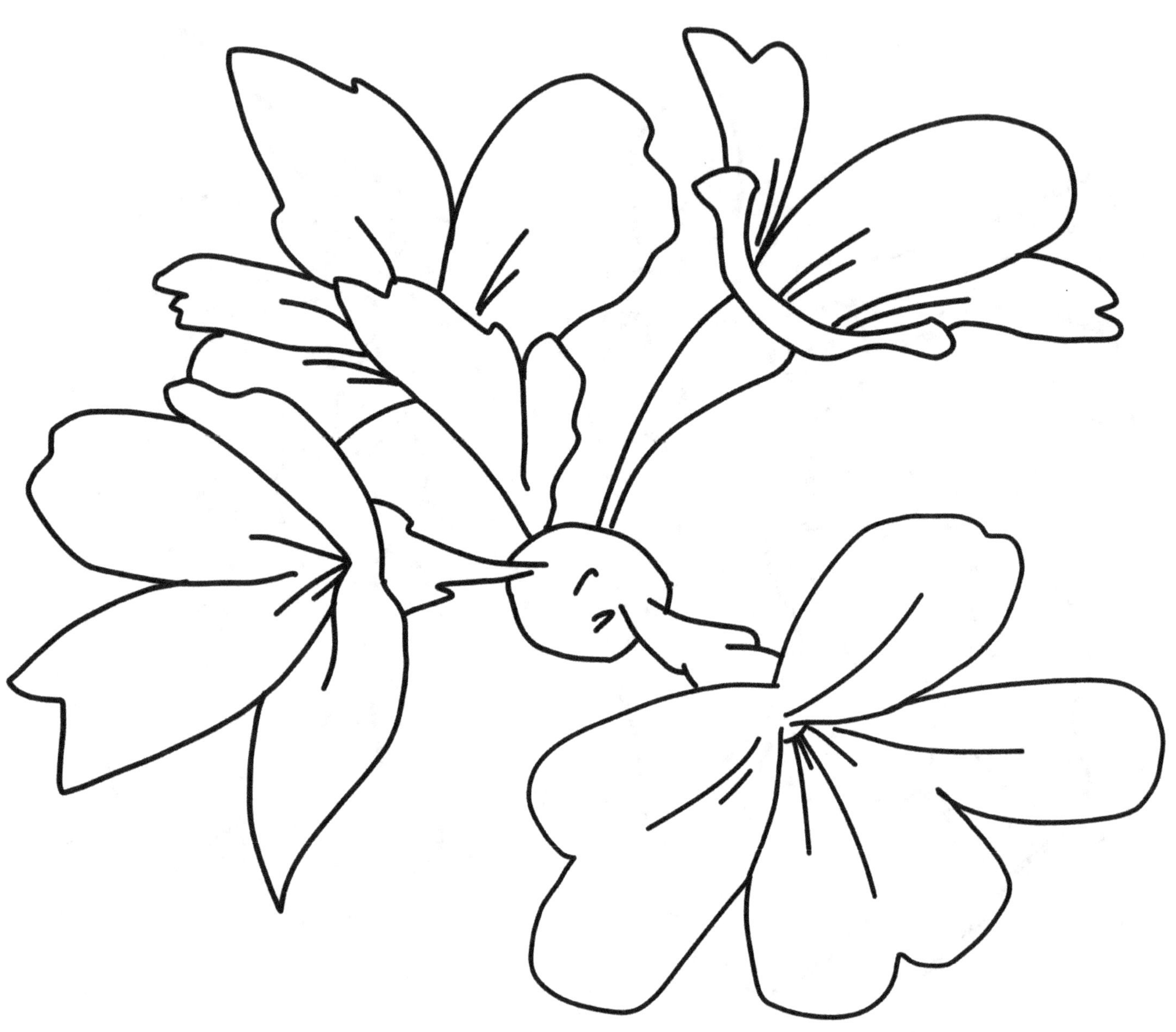

Crossandra is an evergreen, erect sub-shrub
that grows up to 1 meter. It has wavy-margined,
glossy leaves and fan-shaped flowers.

Delonix Regia

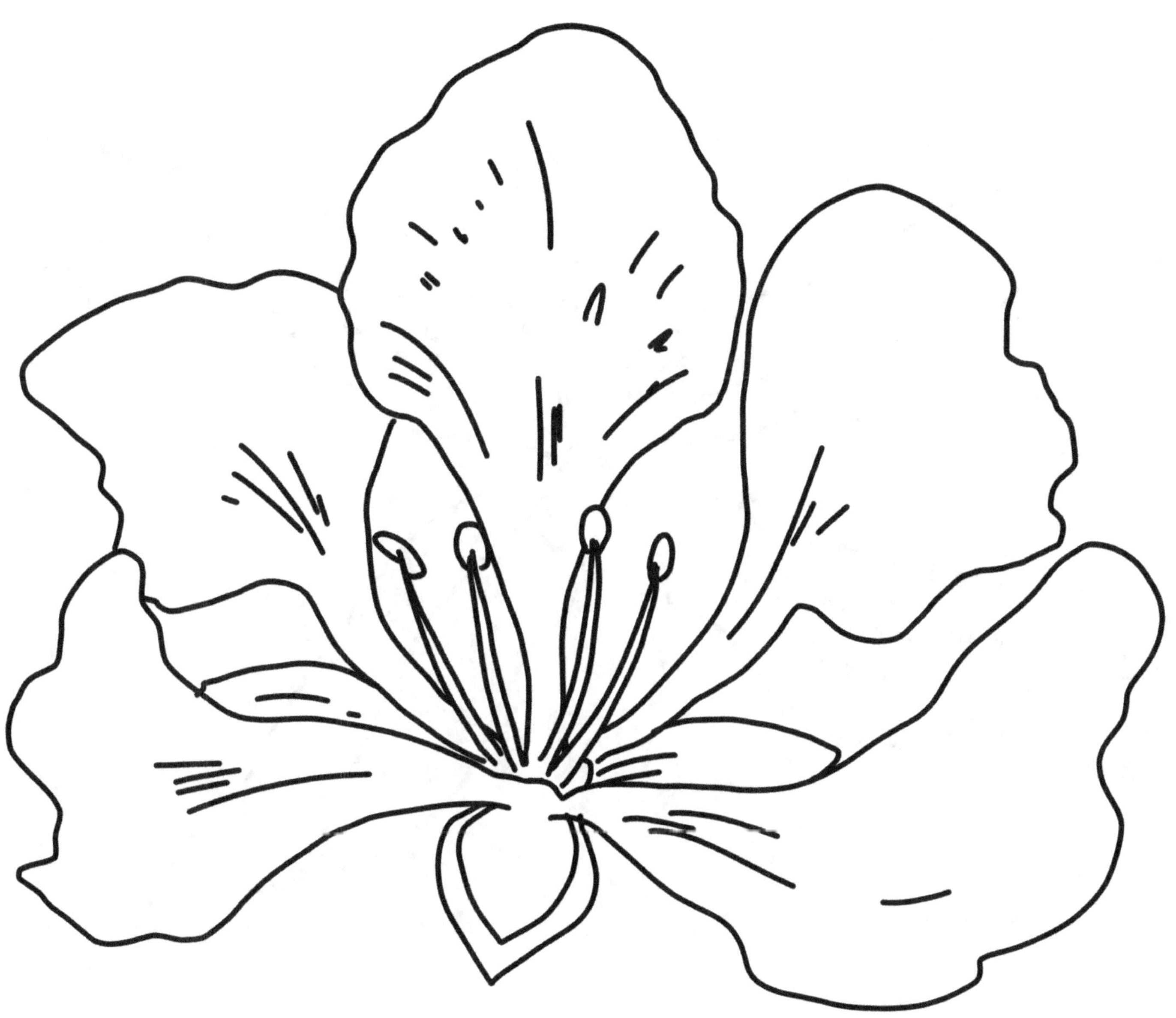

Delonix Regia has fern-like leaves and
a very ornate showcase of orange-red flowers
in the summertime. These are gorgeous flowers.

Euphorbia cyathophor

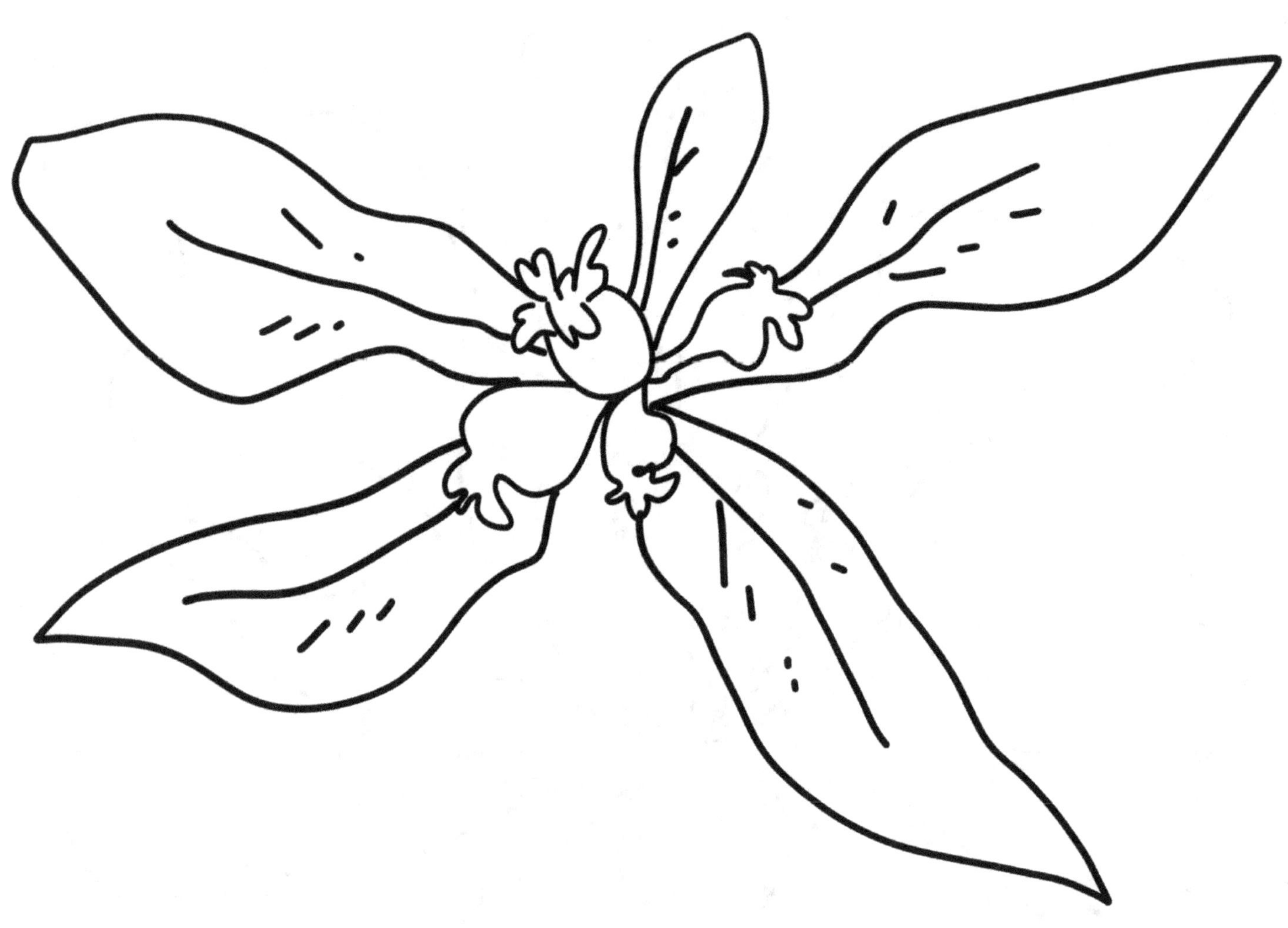

Euphorbia Cyathophora is known by many different names, like, dwarf poinsettia, painted leaf, and fire-on-the-mountain. This flower is native to North India and North & South America.

Forest Ghost

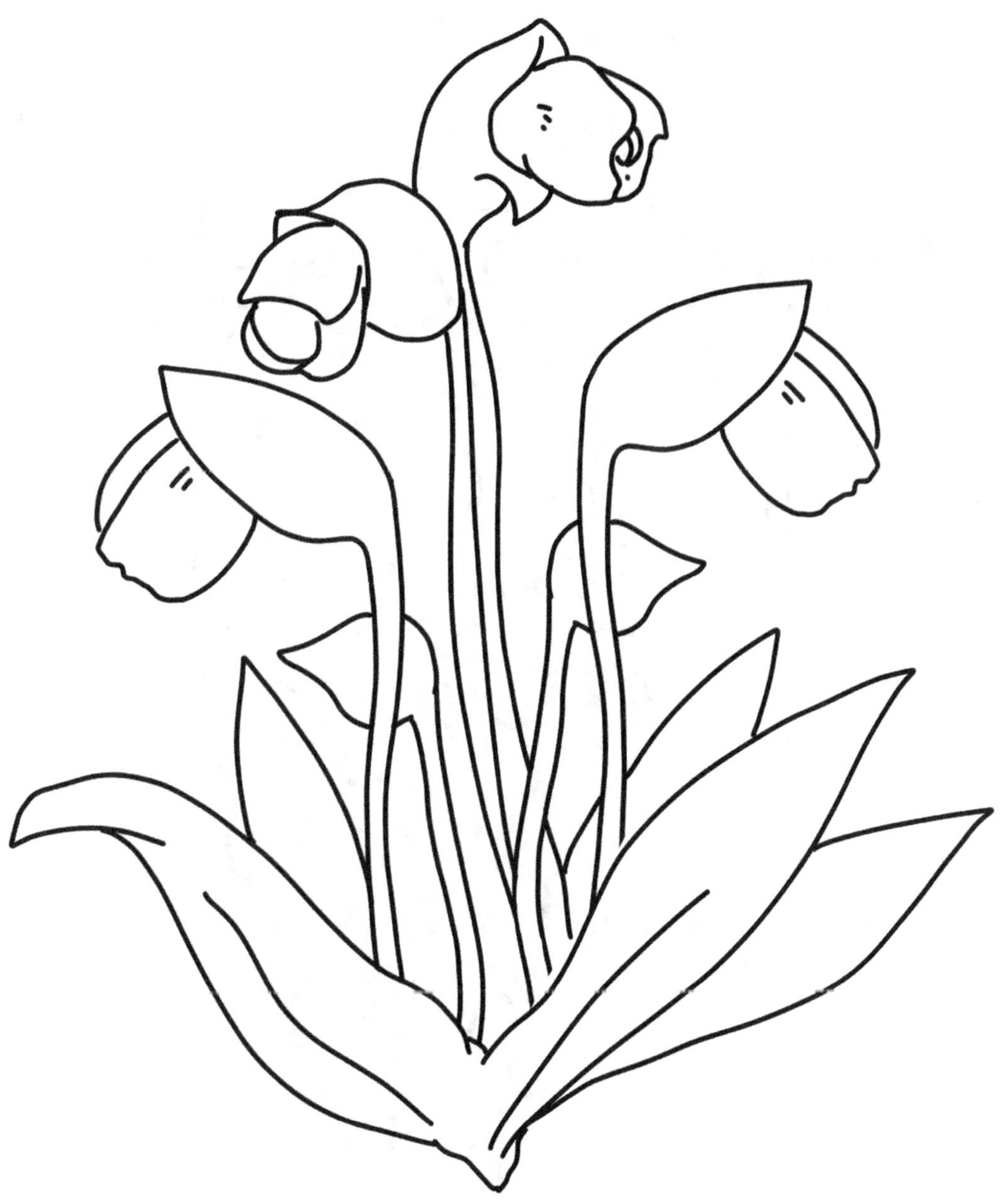

Forest Ghost is a perennial wildflower that grows in the US, from Maine to California and from Florida to Alaska. It takes energy from other plants.

Golden Shower

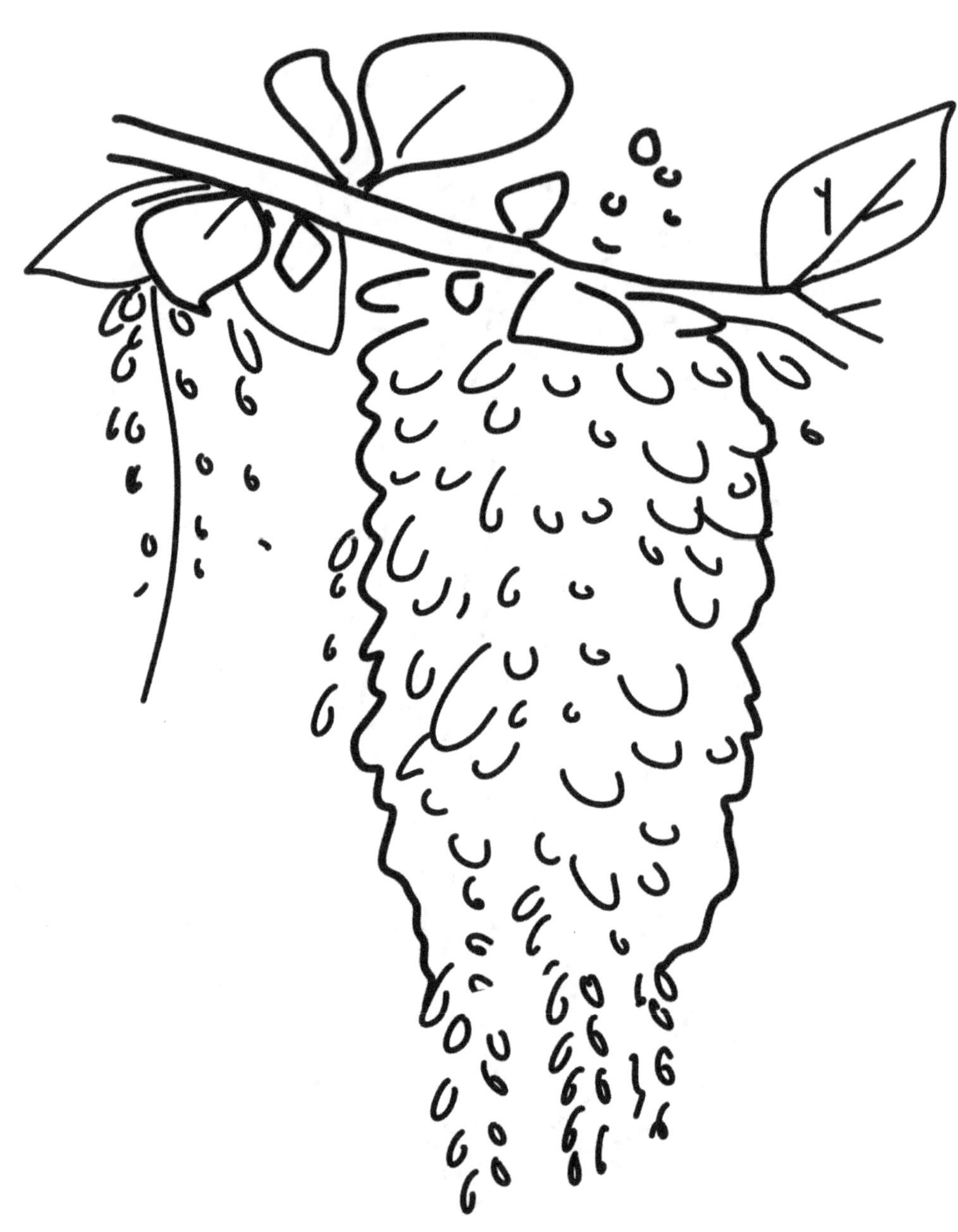

Golden Shower species is native to the
Indian subcontinent. It is a very popular
ornamental plant. It is used in herbal medicine.

Hypericum

Hypericum flower has hundred different varieties. They can be found in different colours. The flower is also commonly known as "St. John Wort".

IxoraCoccinea

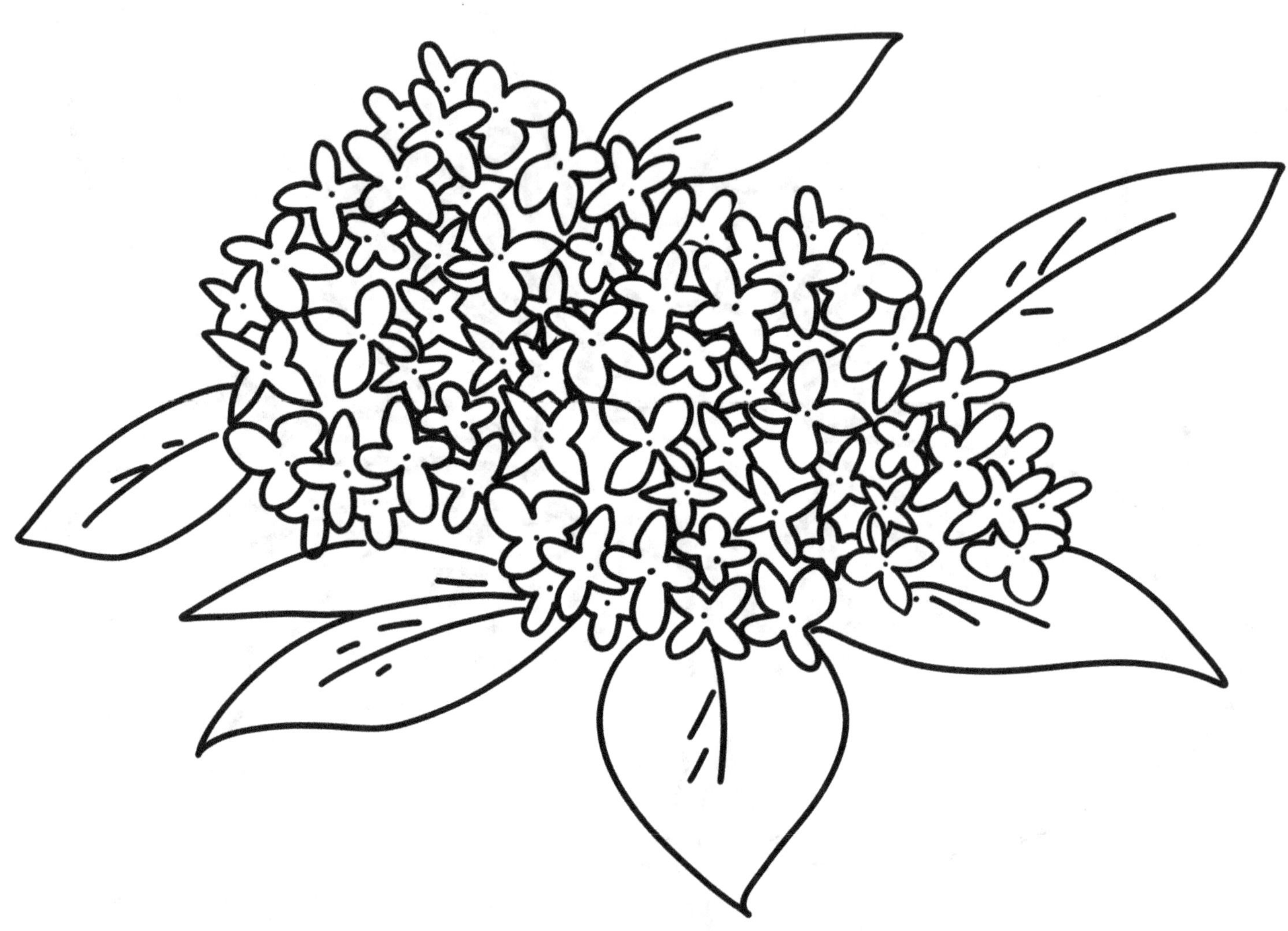

The plant of this flower is native to tropical Asian regions.
It can grow from 0.6 meters to 3.6 meters in height.
These usually have glossy, medium to dark green leaves.

Jasmine

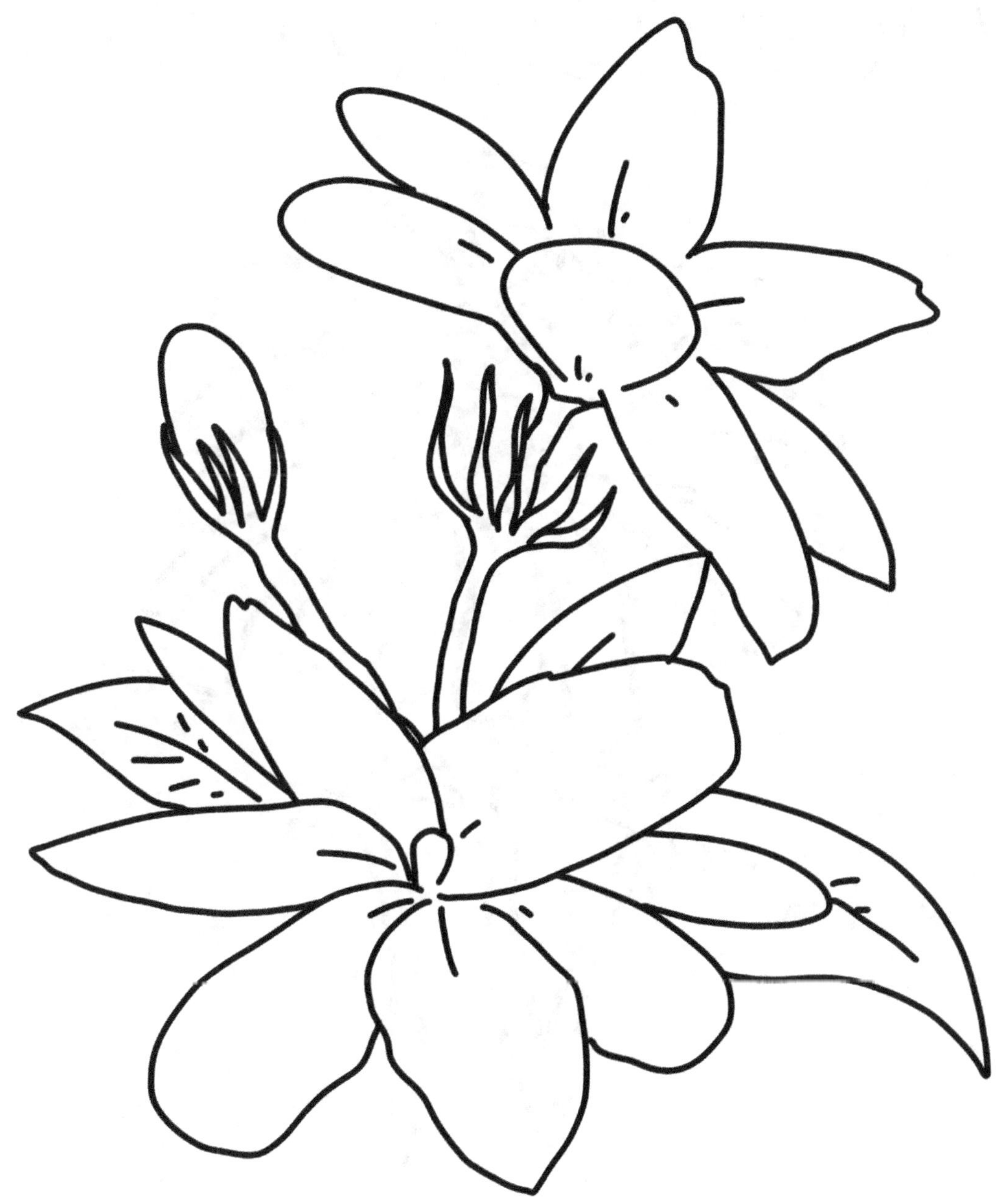

Majority species of Jasmine grows as climbers on other structures or plants. These are white colored flowers, but some species can be yellow also.

Knautia Macedonica

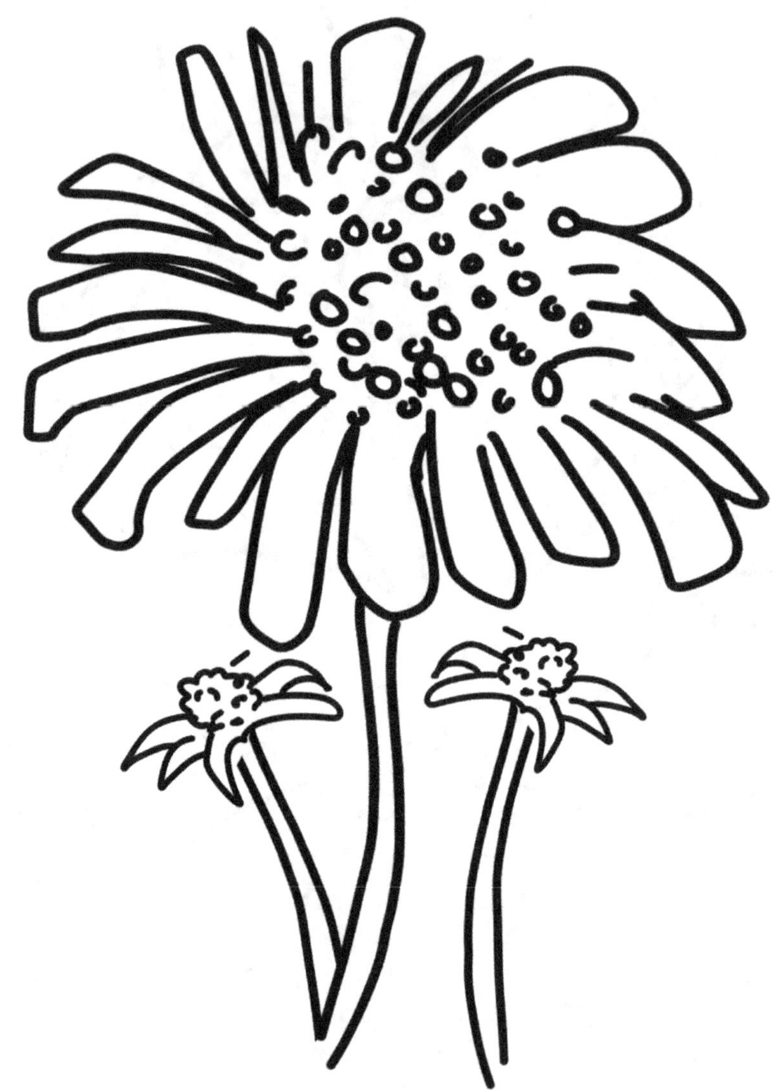

Knautia Macedonica is easy to grow. It is also low maintenance. To grow a Knautia Macedonica, all one needs is a little water, well-drained soil and sun.

Lotus

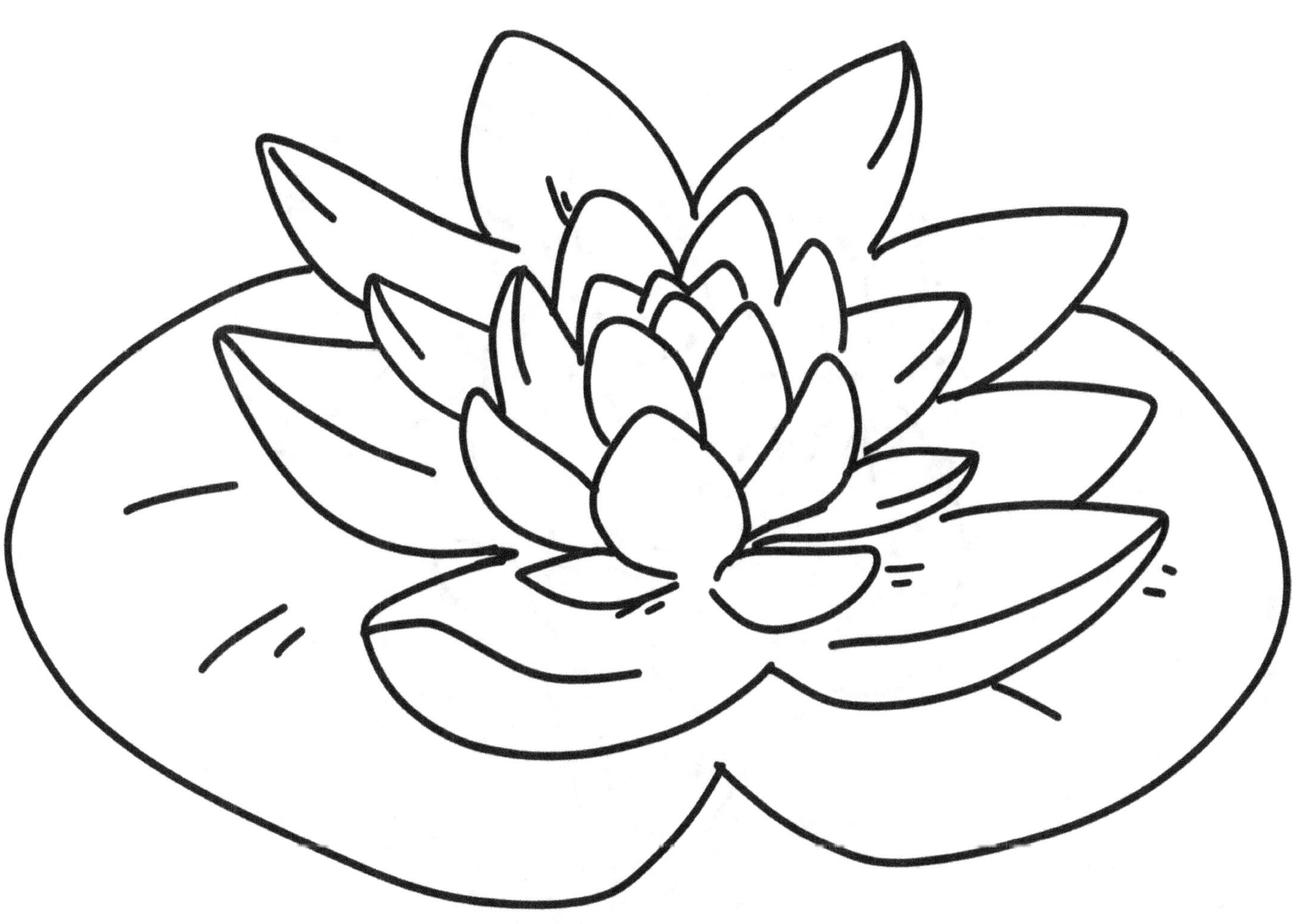

Lotus is an aquatic flower. It grows in freshwater.
It floats on lakes and ponds. It has boat-shaped petals.
They are usually pink in colour,
but white lotus can also be found.

Millingtonia Hortensis

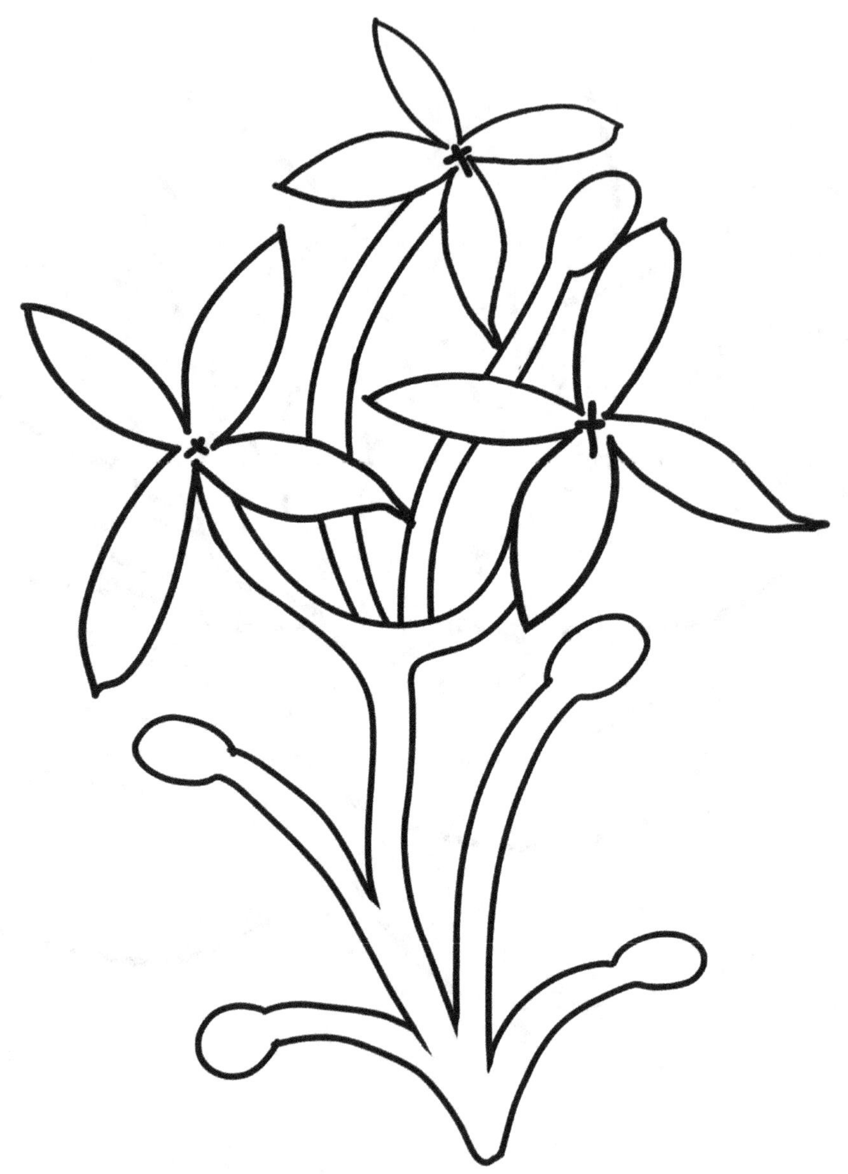

The common name for Millingtonia Hortensis is the Indian cork tree or tree Jasmine. Its unique fragrance is the first thing that one notices in it.

Night Flowering Jasmine

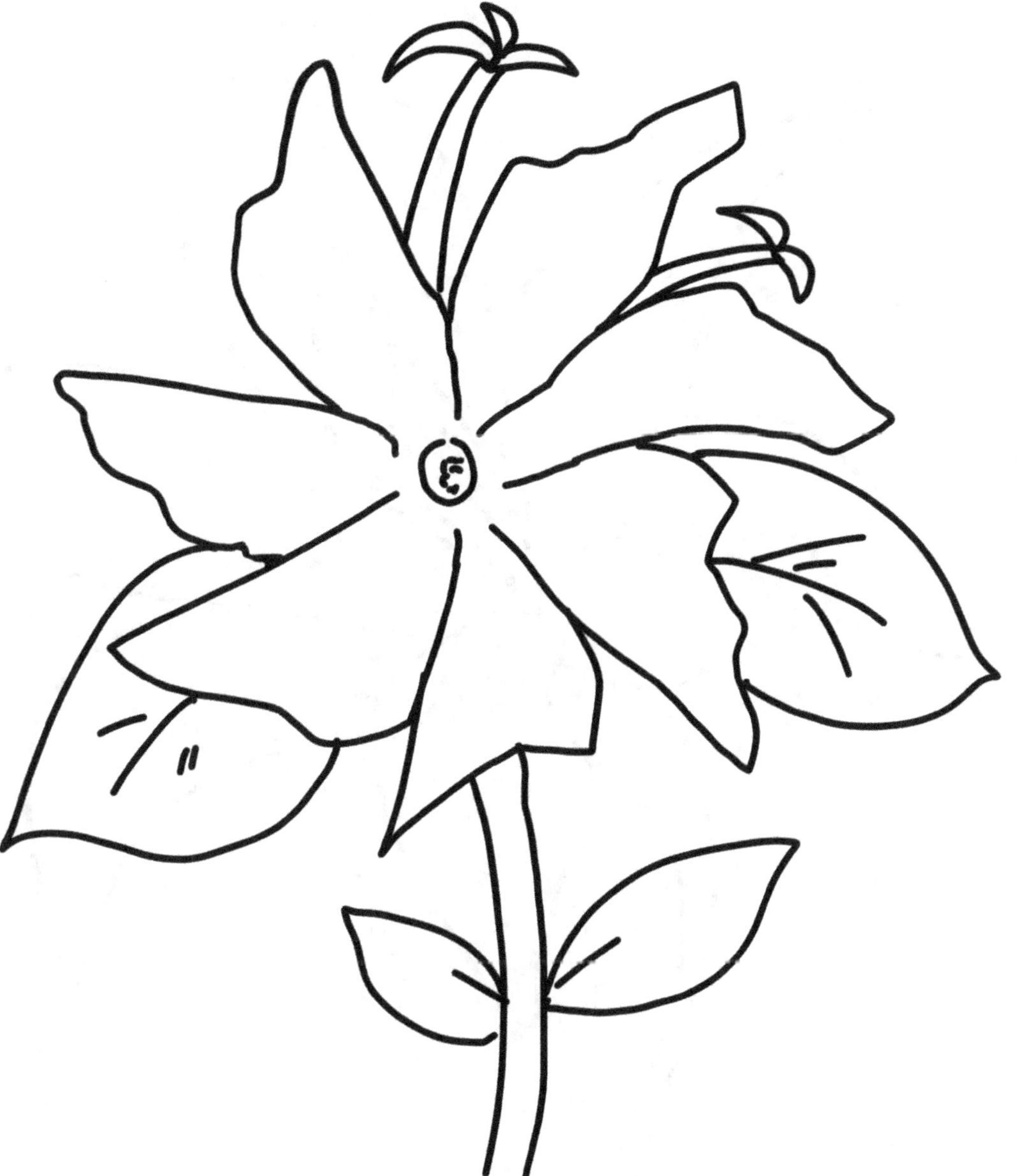

Night Flowering Jasmine grow in cluster on the plant. These are small, white-green flowers that grow during the spring season through late summers.

Orange Tiger Lily

Orange Tiger Lily is a large orange flower with dark spots on the petals. It can grow up to 3" across. It has a powerful, sweet scent.

Peacock Flower

The other common names of Peacock Flower are Dwarf Poinciana and Pride of Barbados. These resemble the Gulmohar tree, only that the plant height grows only up to 3 meters.

Queen Crape Myrtle

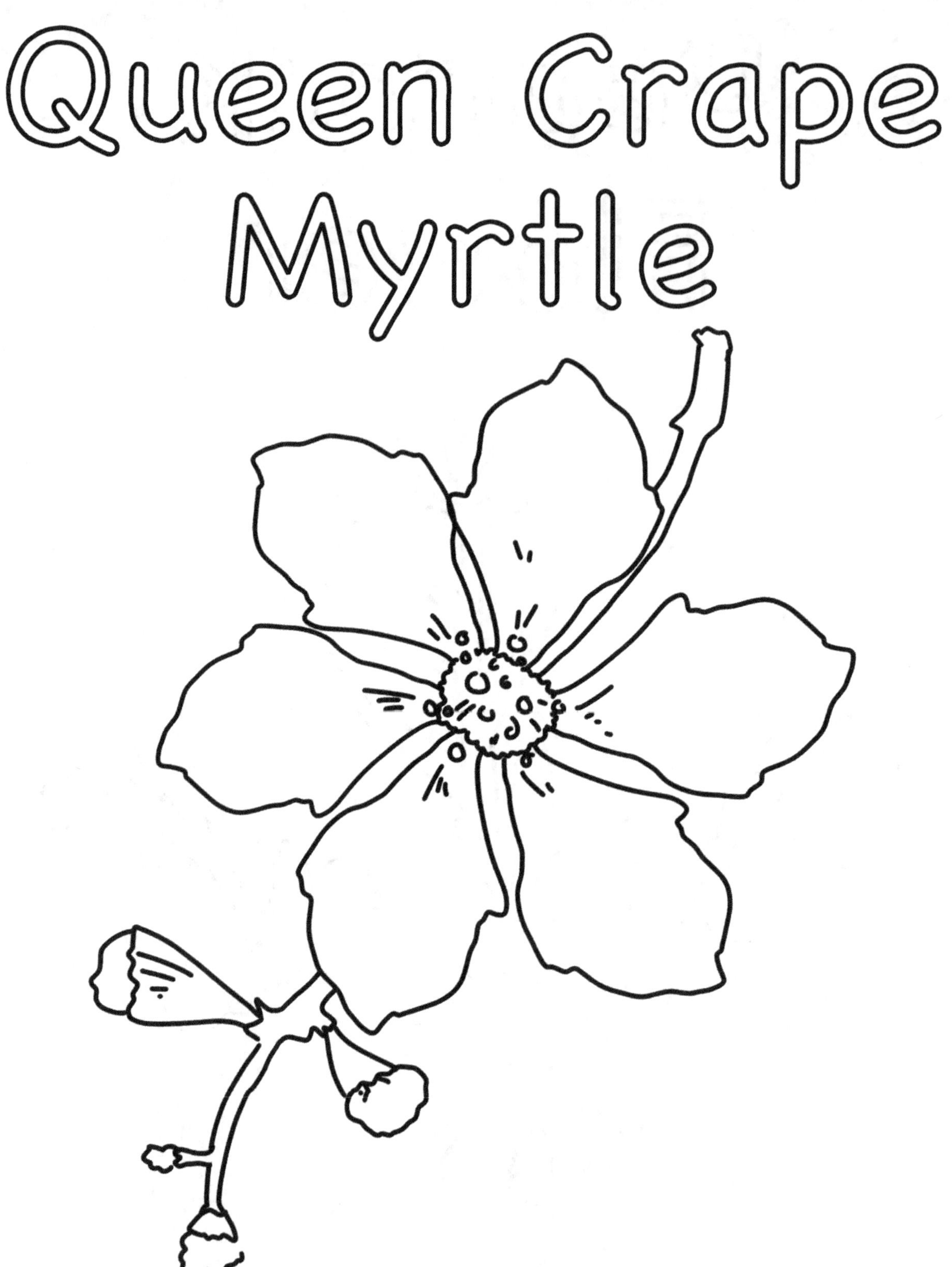

These are beautiful pink flowers that have wrinkled petals resembling crepe paper. It is a safe flower, not poisonous for animals or humans.

Ranunculus Flower

Ranunculus flower or buttercups have yellow, shiny petals. These grow wild in many places. Ranunculus flower is poisonous for cattle and humans.

Showy Rattlepod

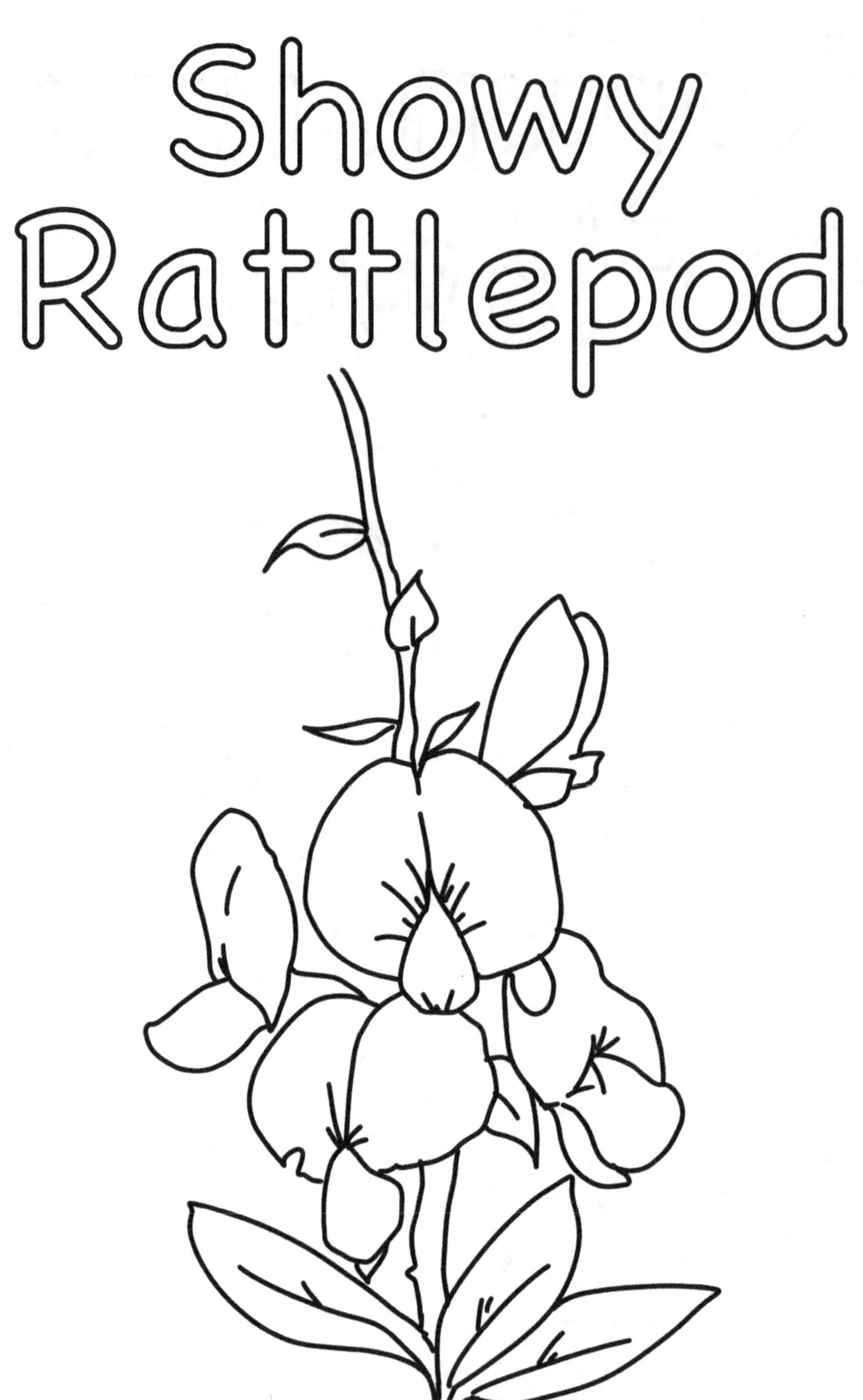

A showy rattle pod is a perennial shrub that grows up to 1.5 meters tall. It has shown traits of harvestability. These are poisonous to livestock, especially the seeds.

Tanners Cassia

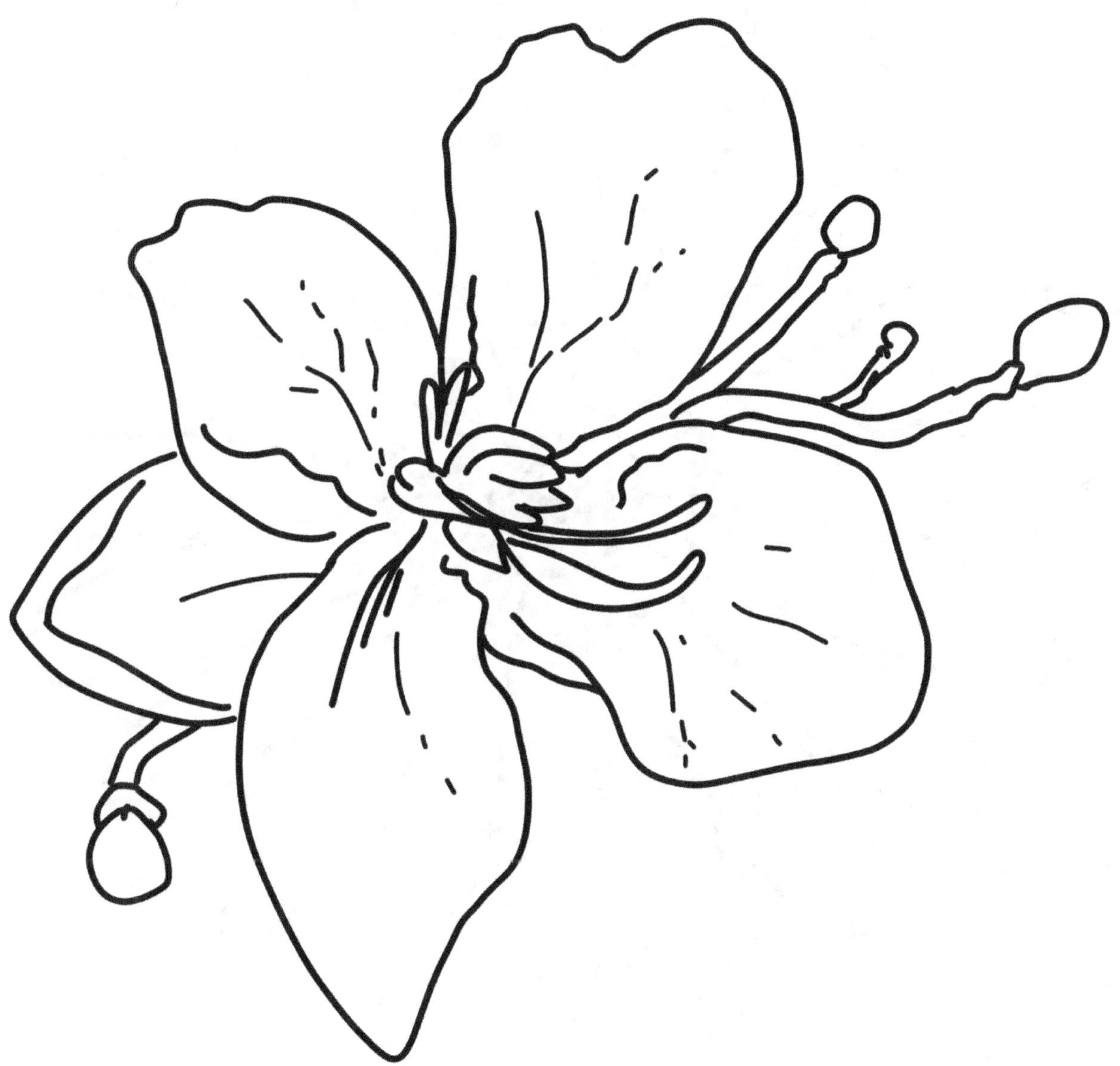

These flowers are famous for their medicinal values, especially in Ayurveda. They are used for eye infections, diabetes, constipation, jaundice, etc.

Ursinia

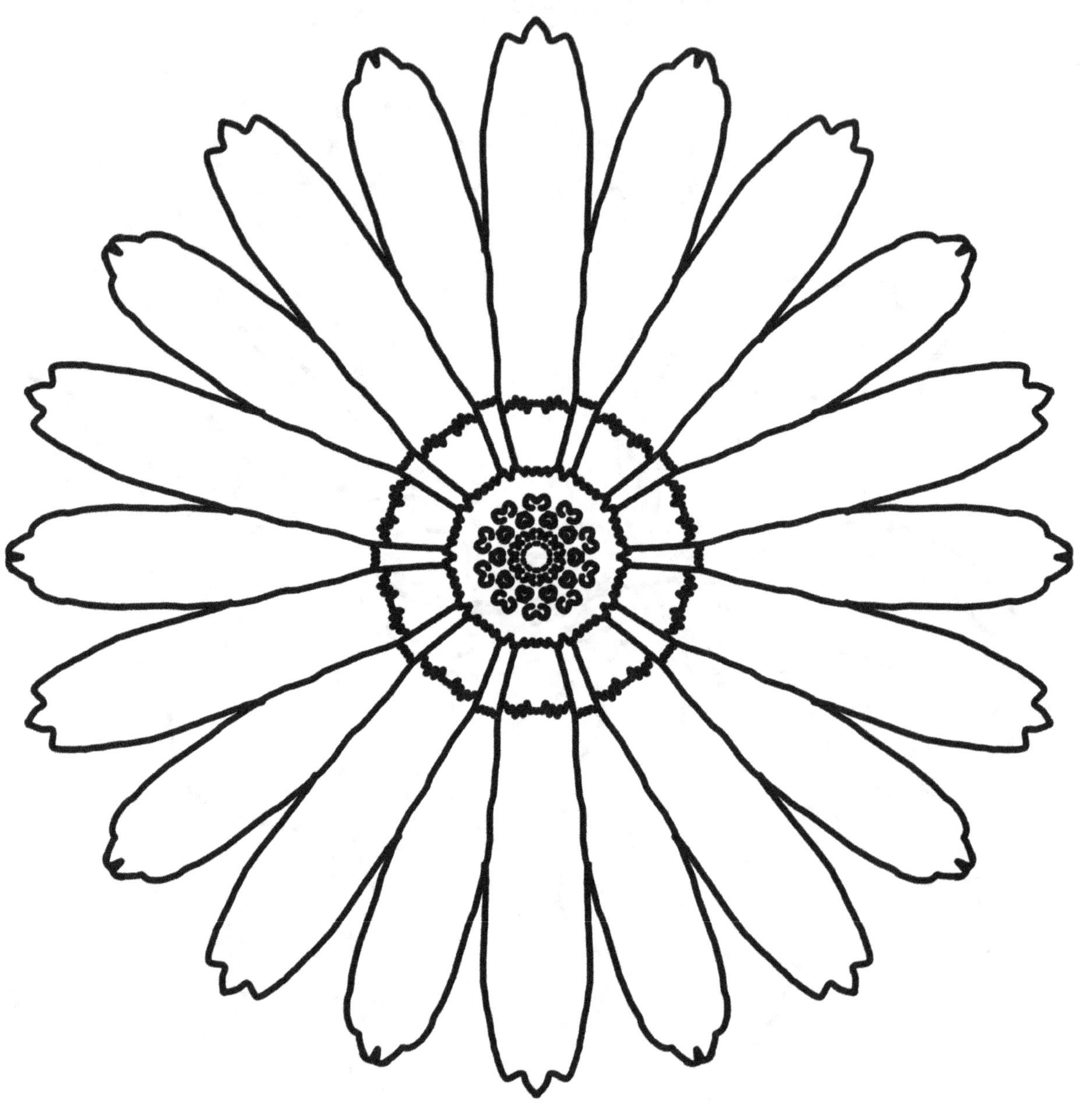

These are easy-to-grow flowers in the South African
region and bloom immensely annually. They are shimmering,
golden and orange in colour.

Vinca minor

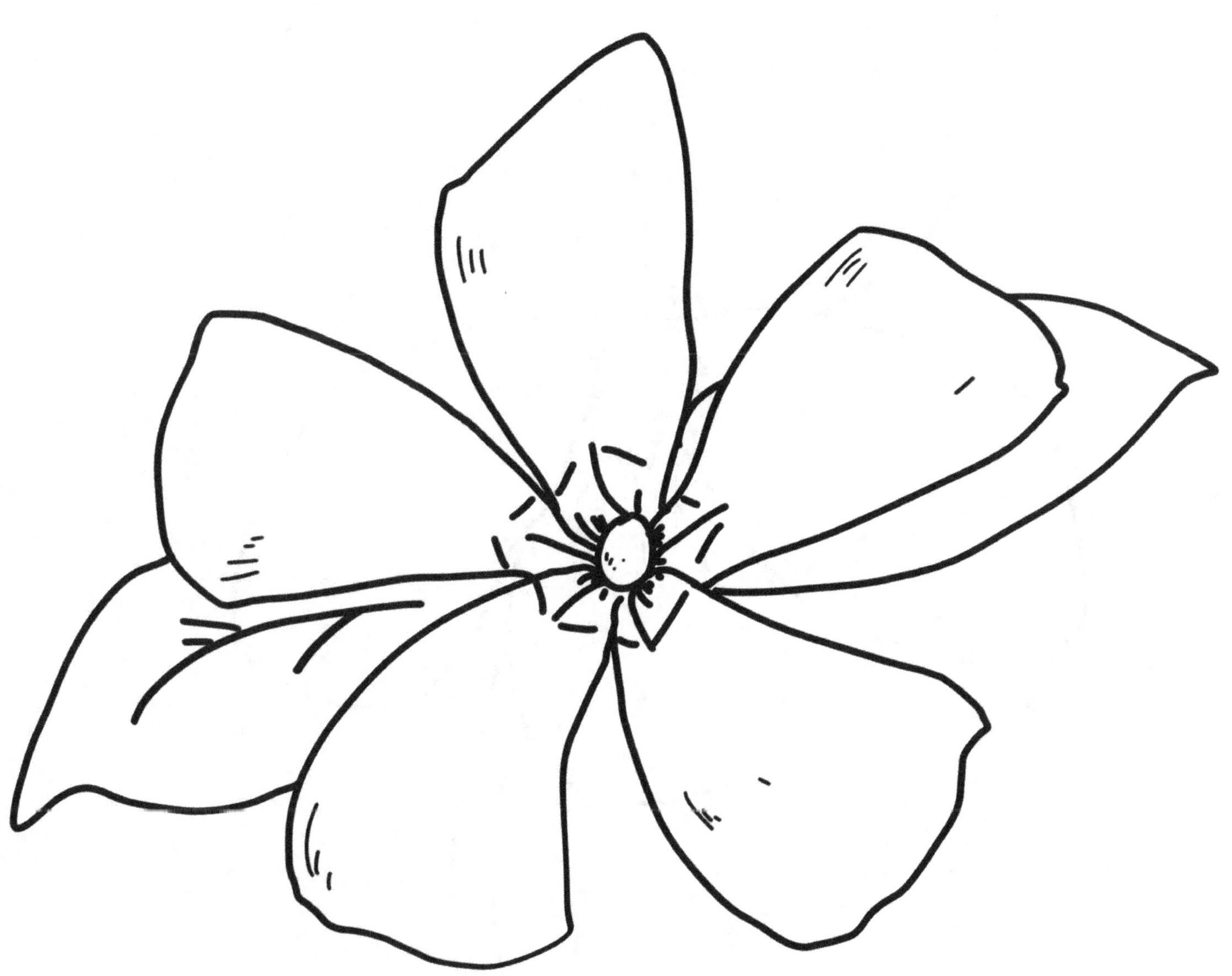

Vinca Minor grows in three different colours-blue, purple or white, depending on the cultivar. These are very ornamental and are used for groundcover.

Woolly Violet

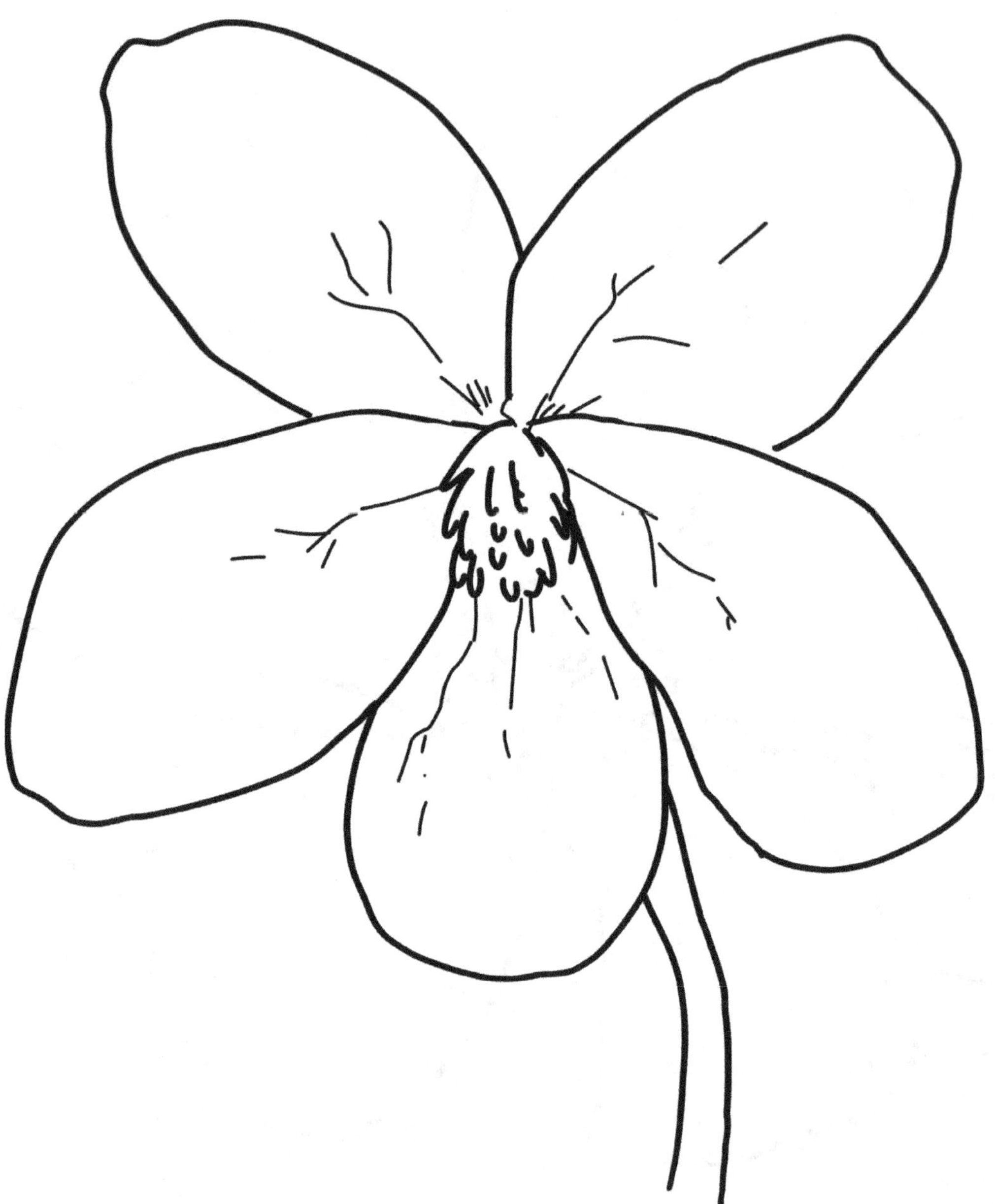

These are delicate flowers that can grow in different colours or combinations of colours. These flowers have five petals and are primarily blue, deep purple or lavender.

Xeranthemum

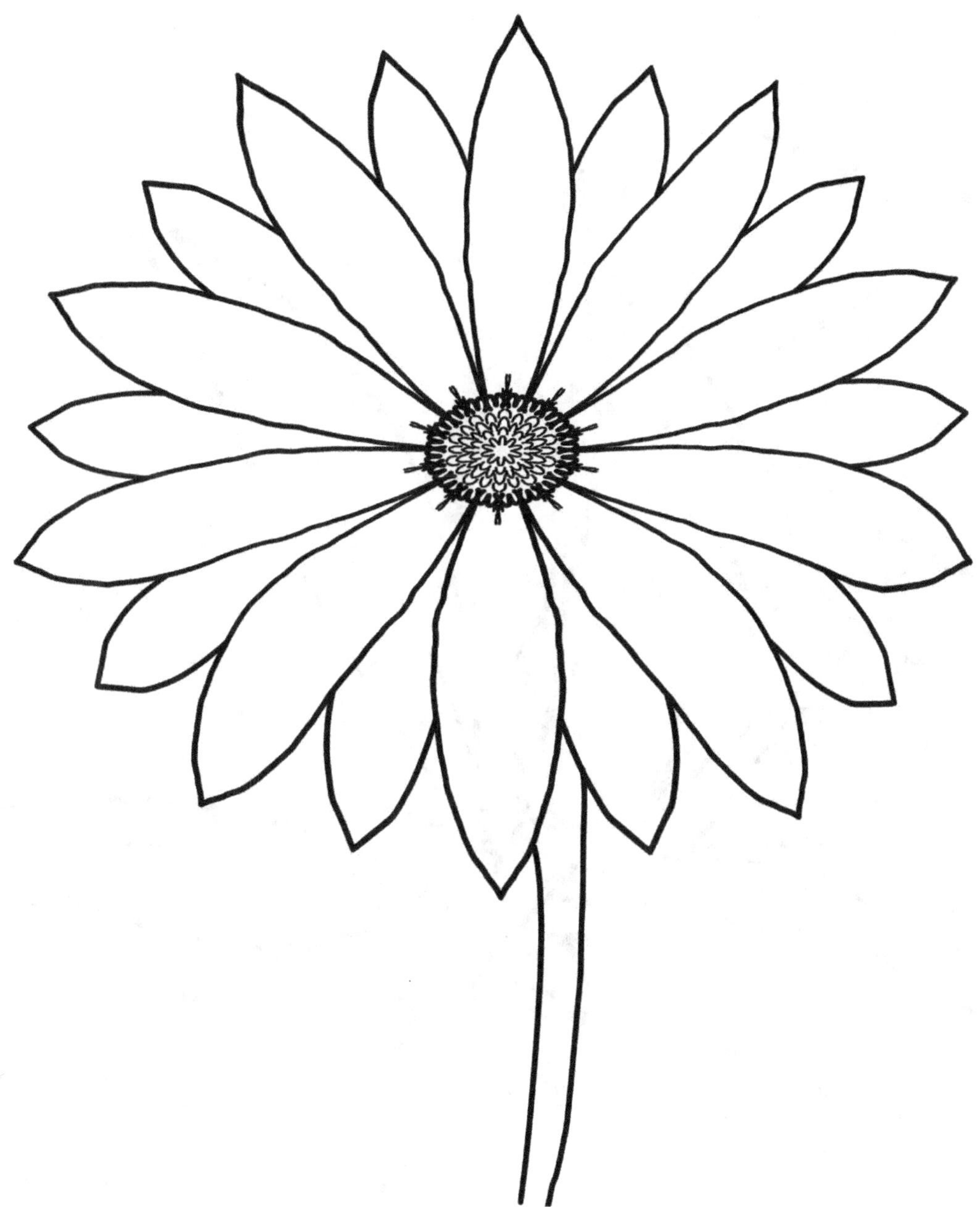

These beautiful flowers are a symbol of
immortality, cheerfulness, everlasting love and eternity.
These are daisy-like papery flowers.

Yellow Oleander

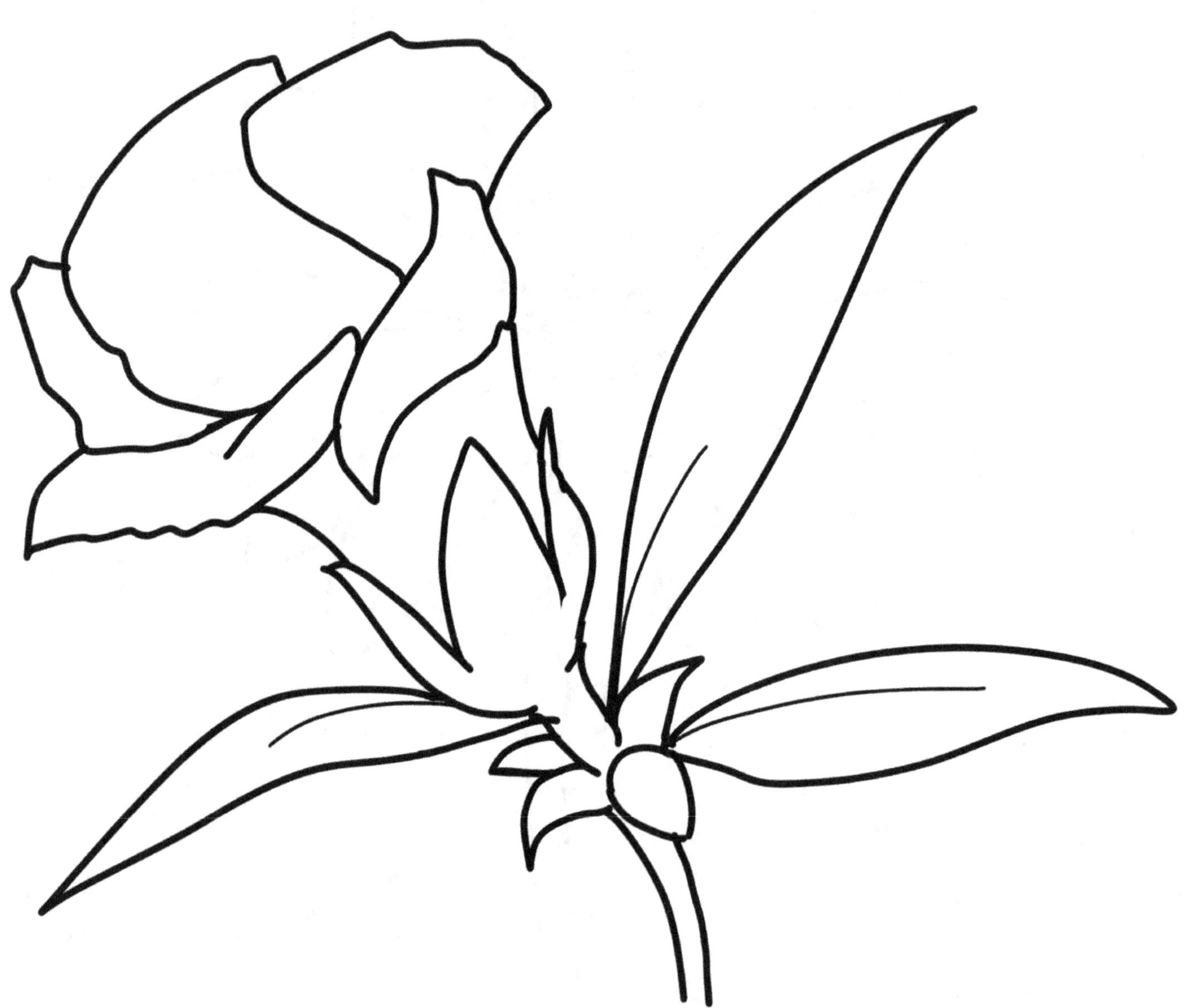

Yellow Oleander is an ornamental tree that commonly grows in tropical regions. The flowers of these trees can be poisonous.

Zinnia elegans

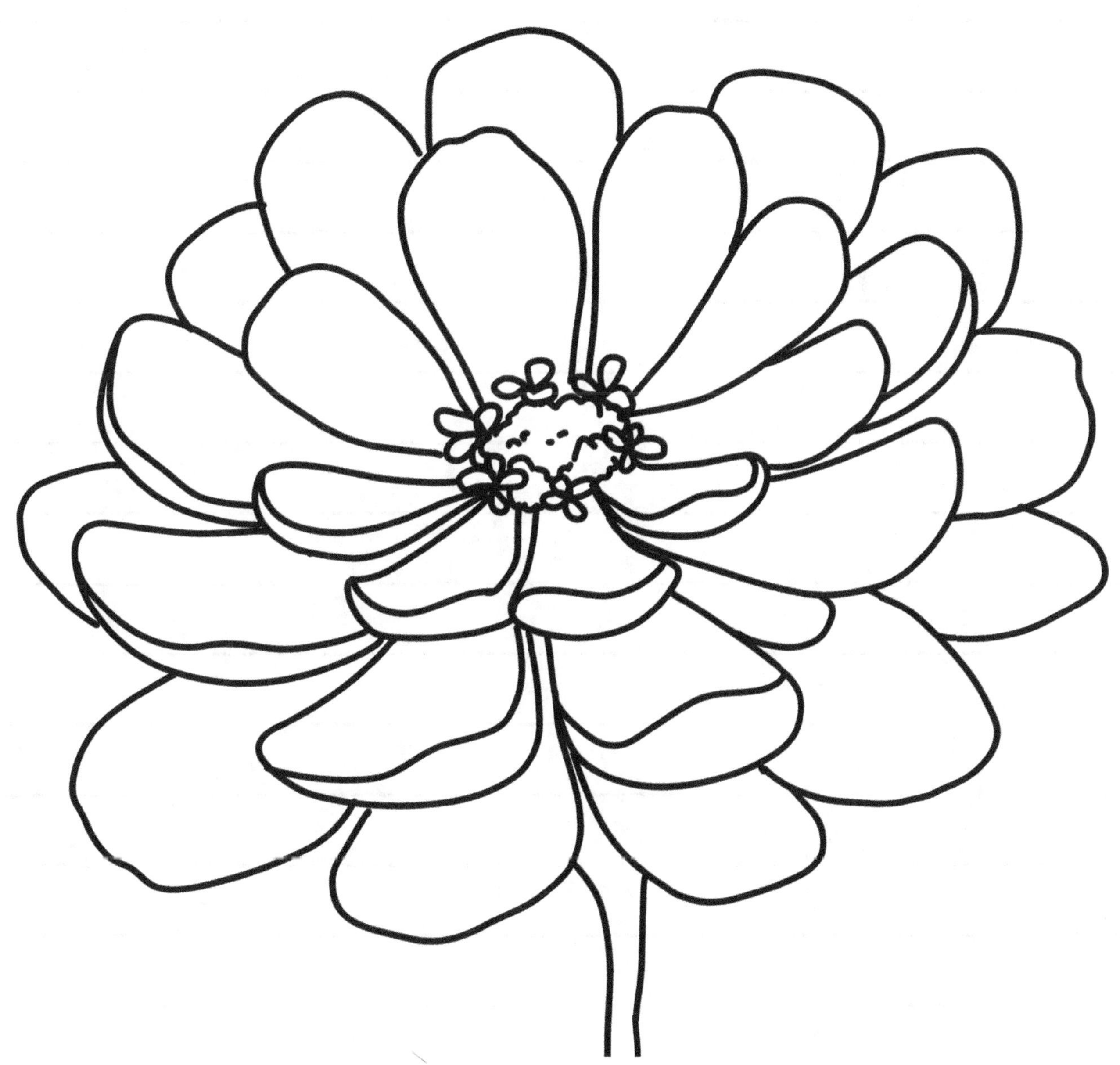

These flowers are available in many
beautiful colours. They can bloom all summer
and can last up to 12 days in a vase.

Name your favorite flower and write a few lines about it

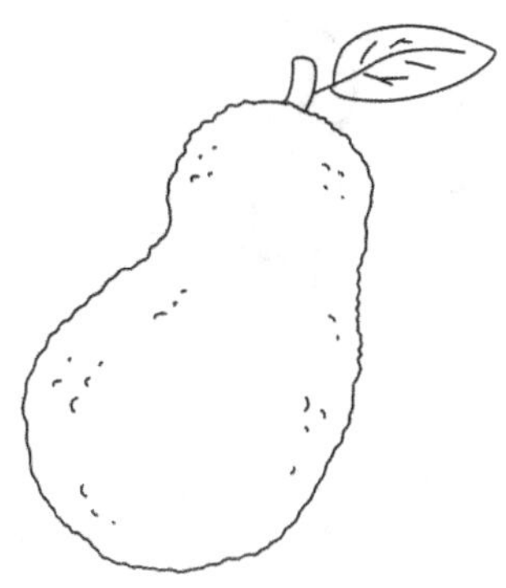

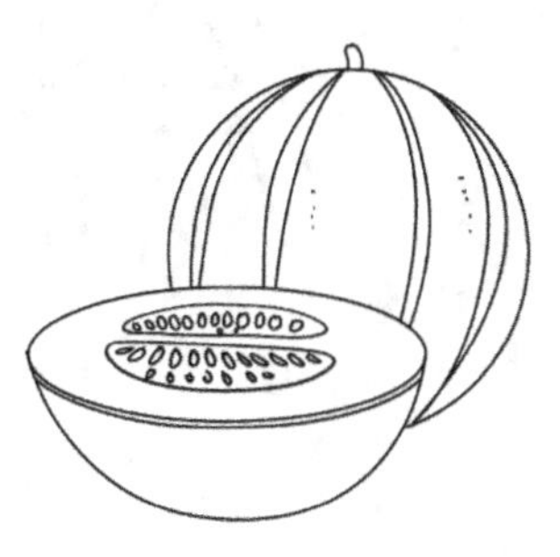

FRUITS AND VEGETABLES

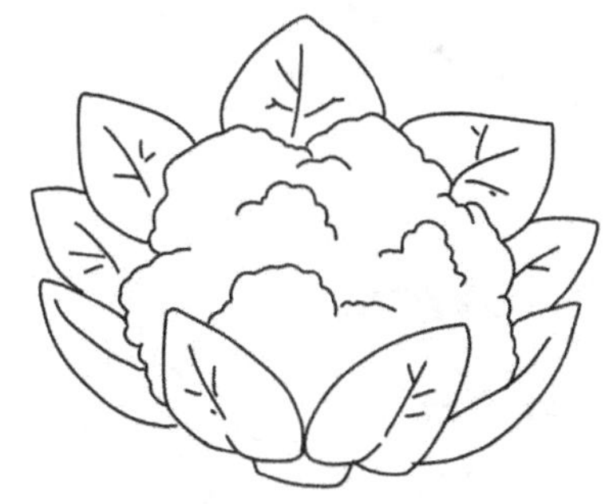

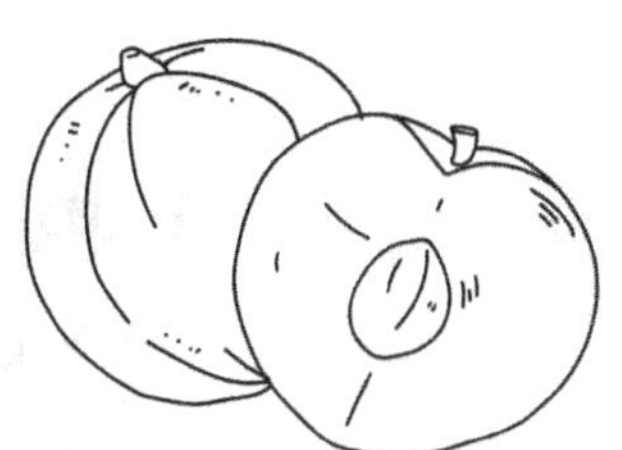

Apples

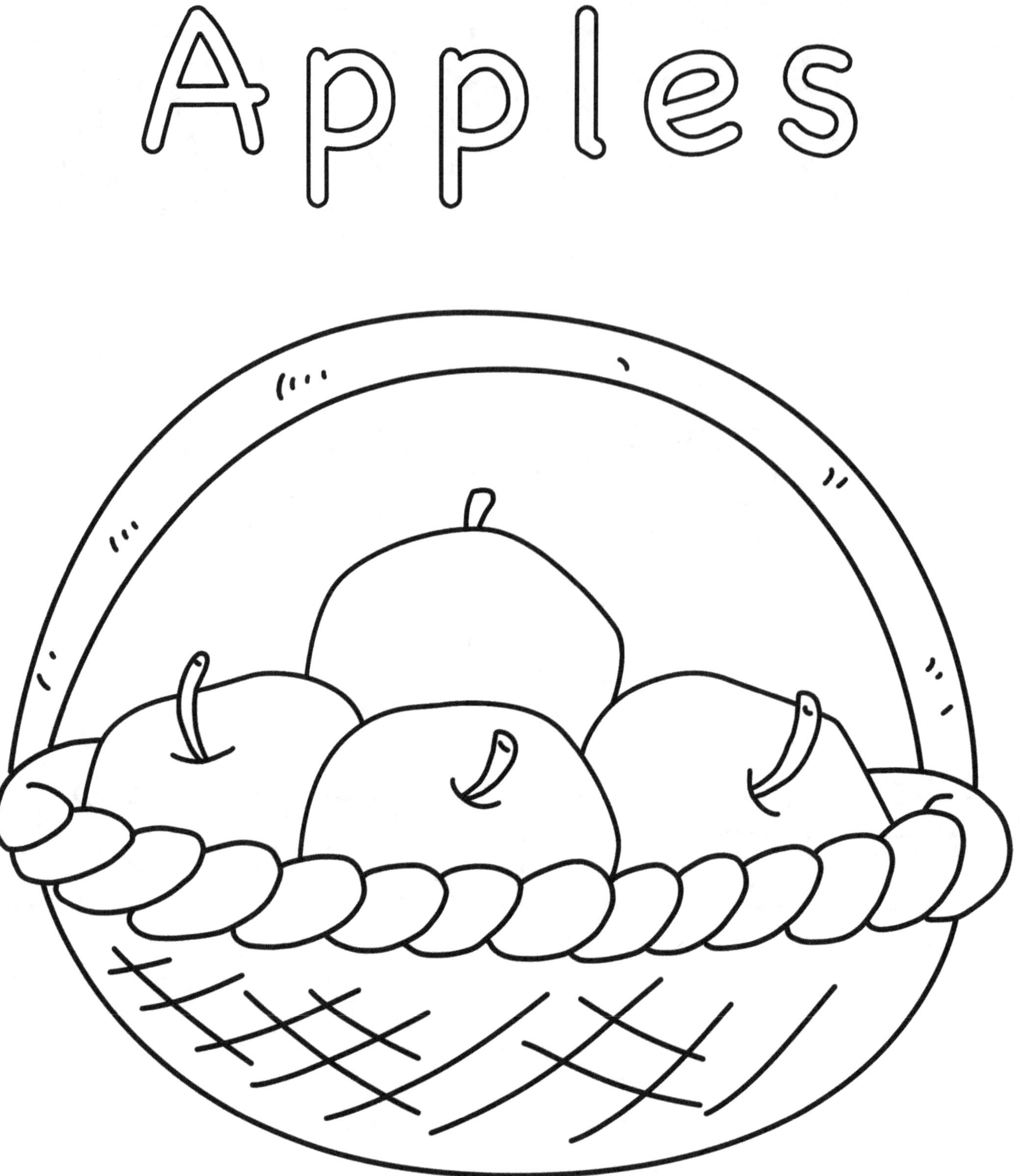

An apple a day keeps the doctors away.
An apple has many health benefits.
It is rich in Vitamin C and many other antioxidants.

Bananas

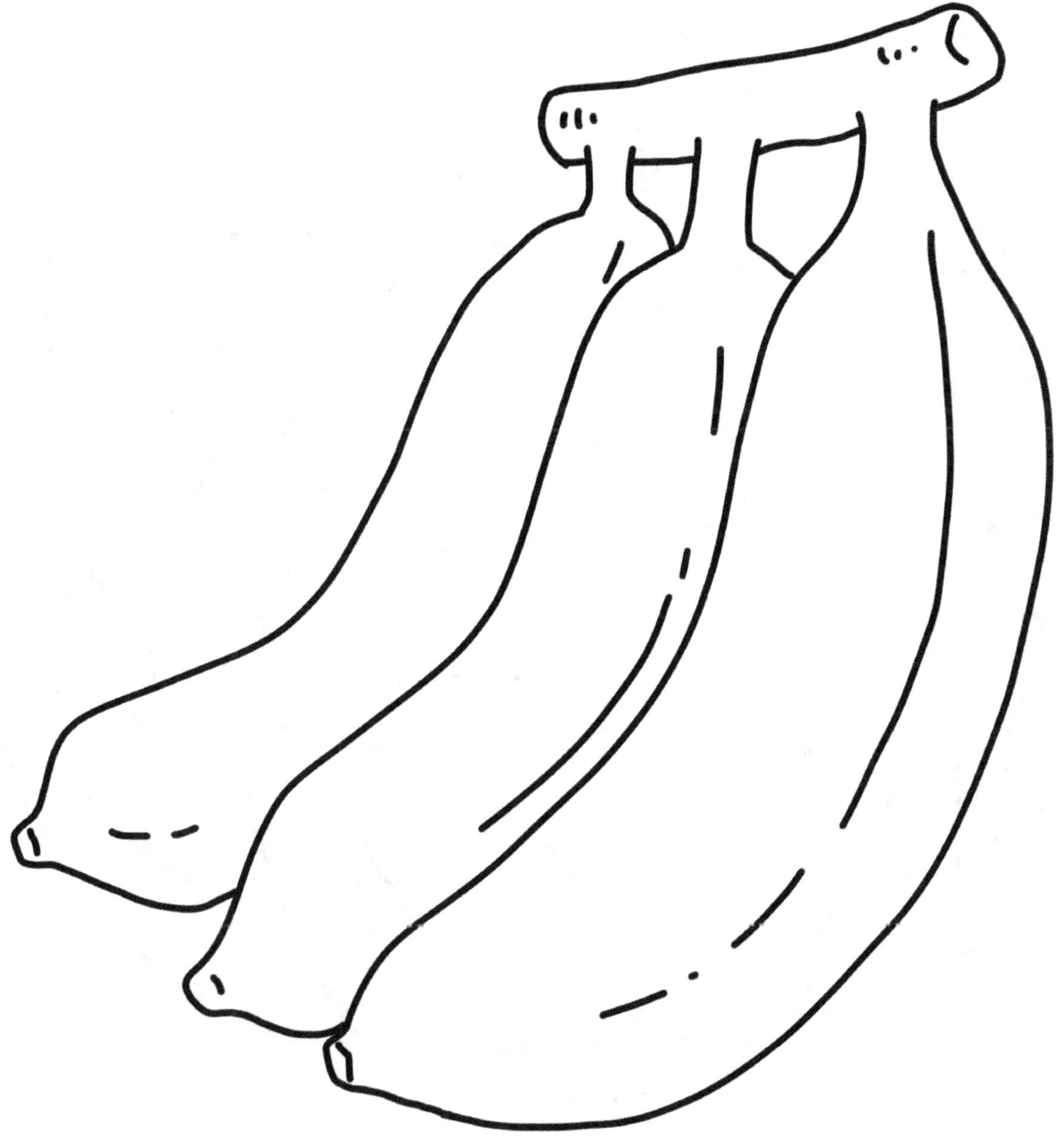

Bananas are long, curved fruit.
These are soft on the inside and have a yellow peel covering.
There also come in different colours, including red.

Cauliflower

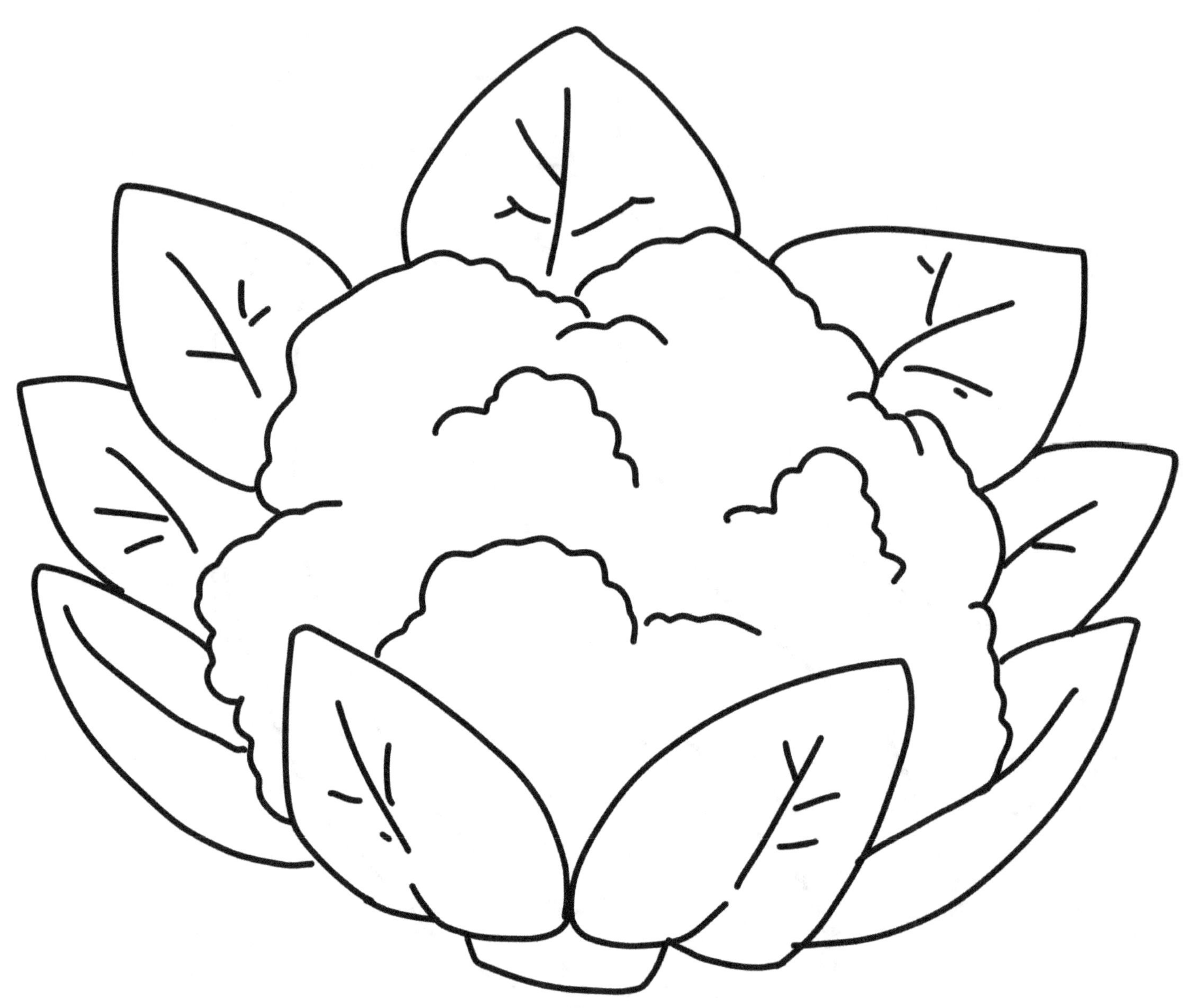

Cauliflower is a flower. The eatable parts of the flower are the flower heads. The leaves are also edible.
It is mainly grown in China.

DragonFruit

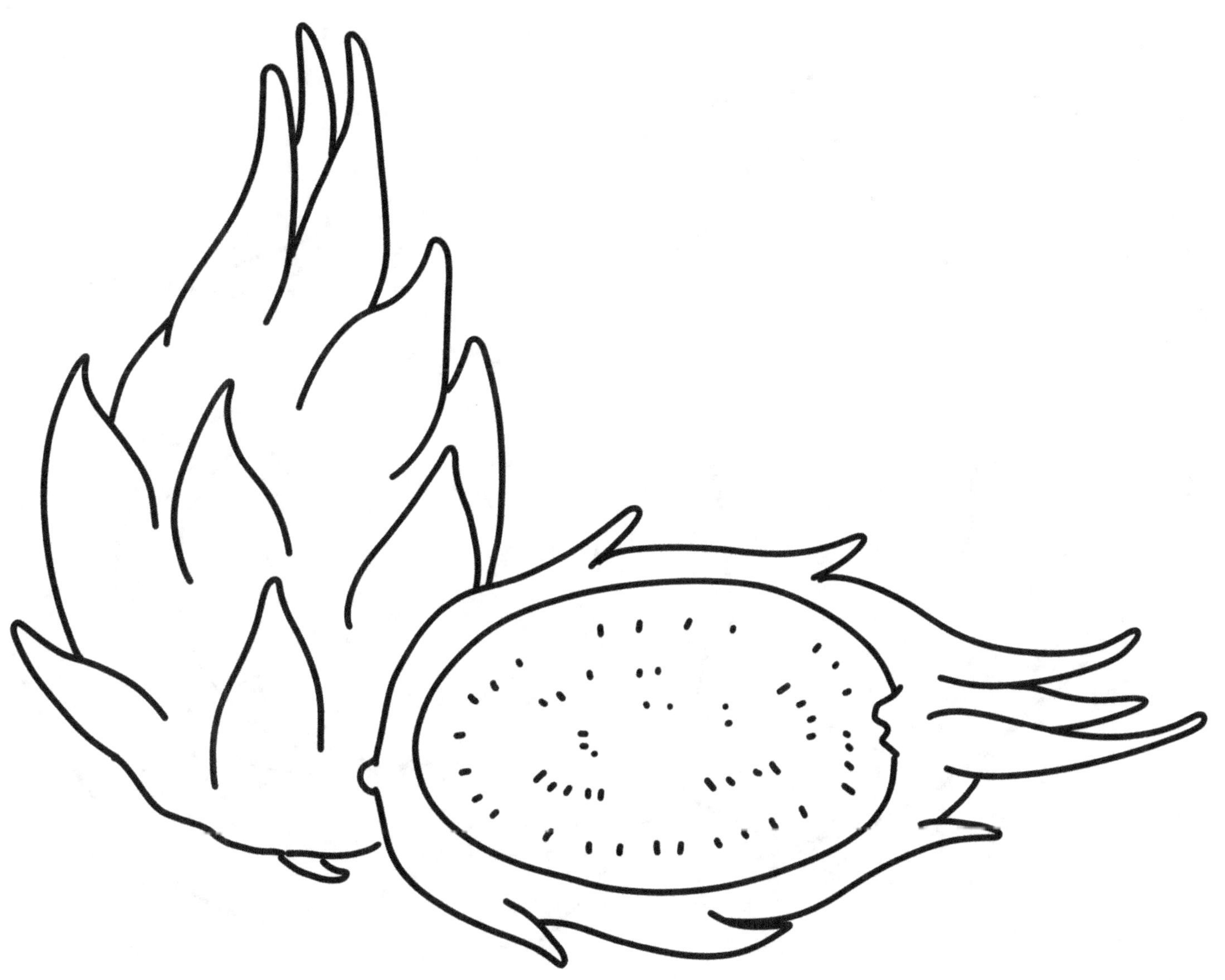

The other name for dragon fruit is "pitaya fruit".
It is commonly grown in South and Central America and Asia.
It has a light, sweet taste.

EggFruit

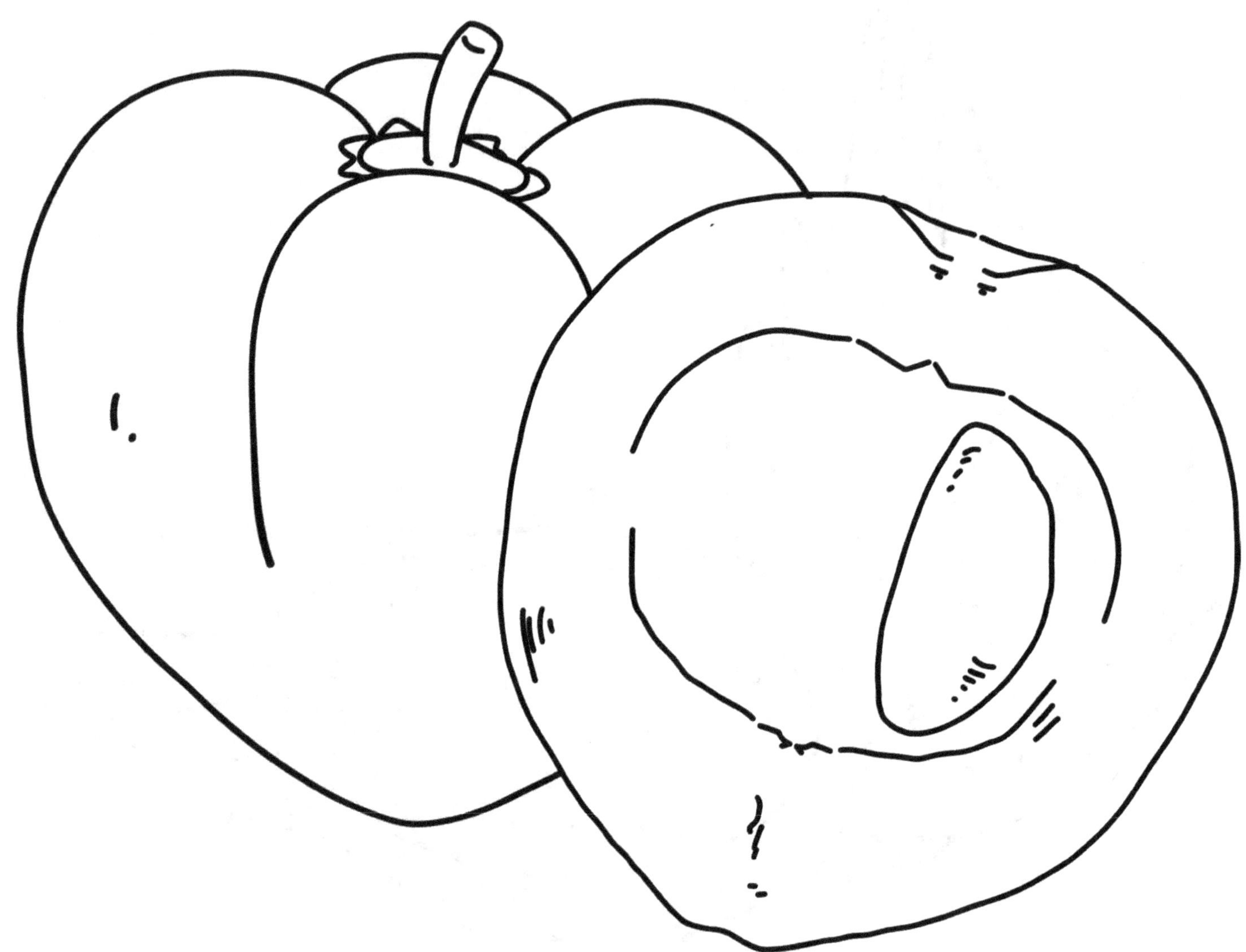

Egg fruits have 1-4 black-brown, hard seeds
that emit a pronounced musky, squash-like scent.
The fruits are naturally sweet in flavour.

Fig

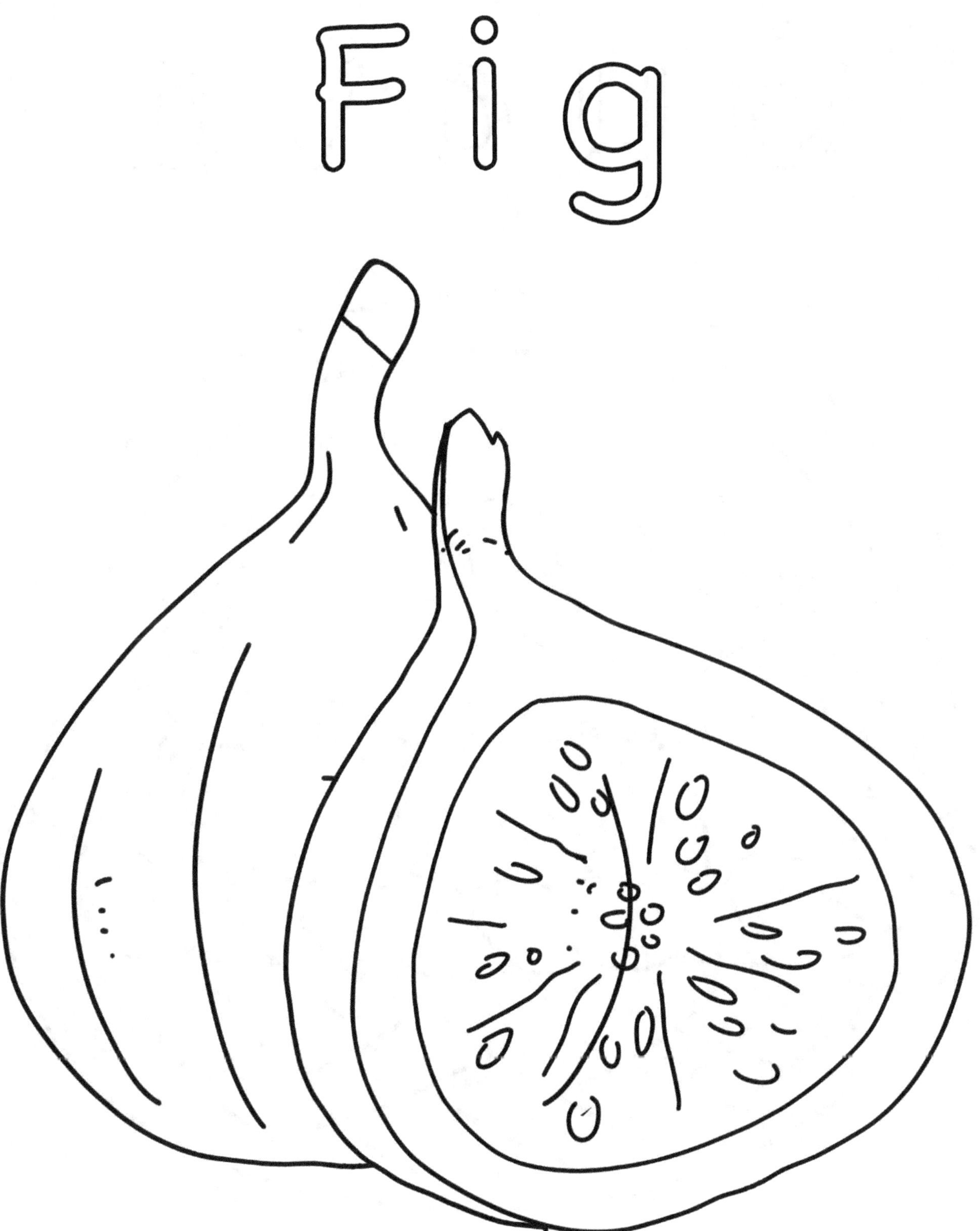

Figs have high sugar content.
They're also rich in soluble fibre and minerals.
These fruits are a good source of antioxidants.

Guava

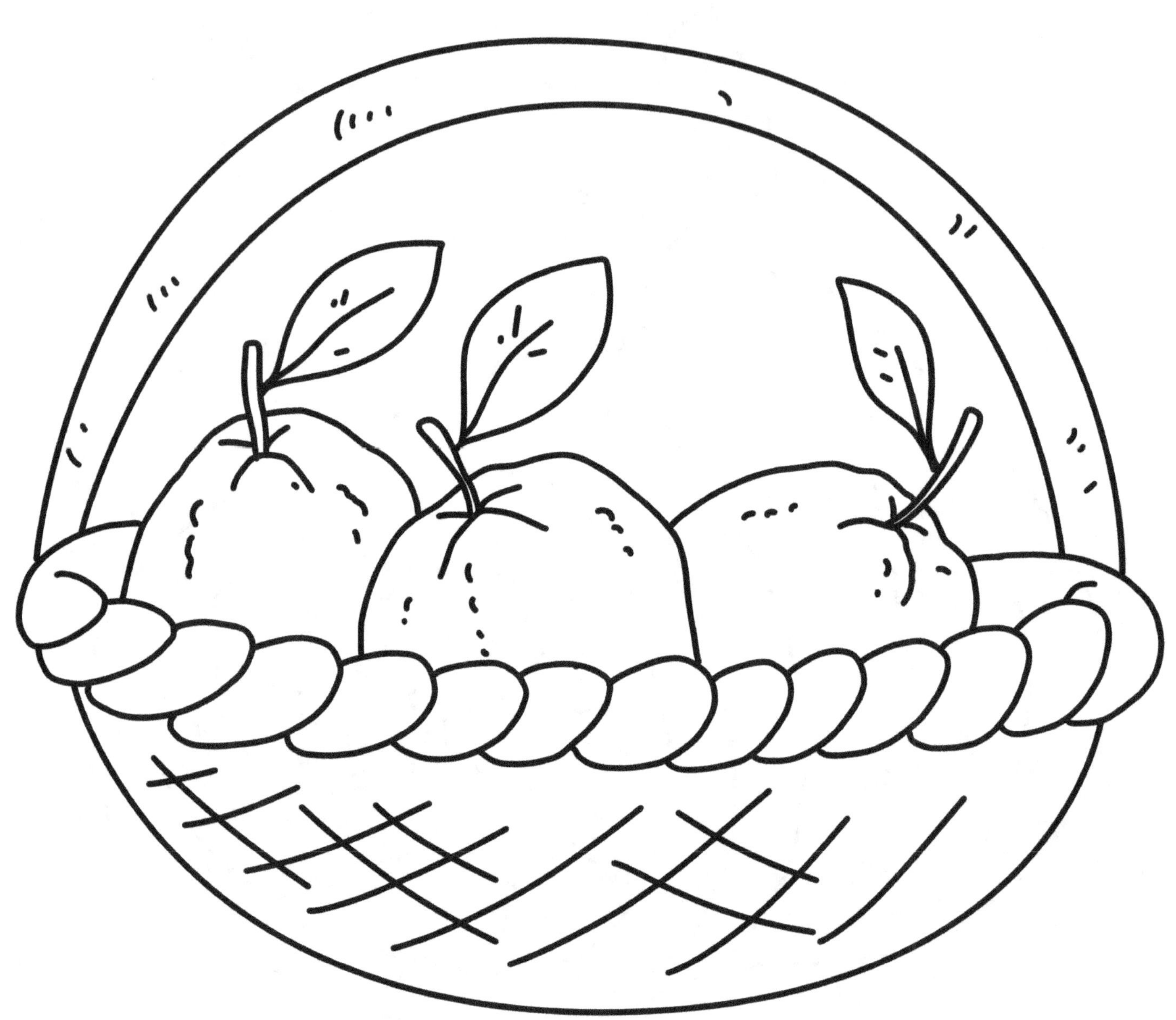

Guava is round to pear-shaped.
They are yellow on the outside.
The flesh of Guava can be pink, yellow or white.

Honey Dew

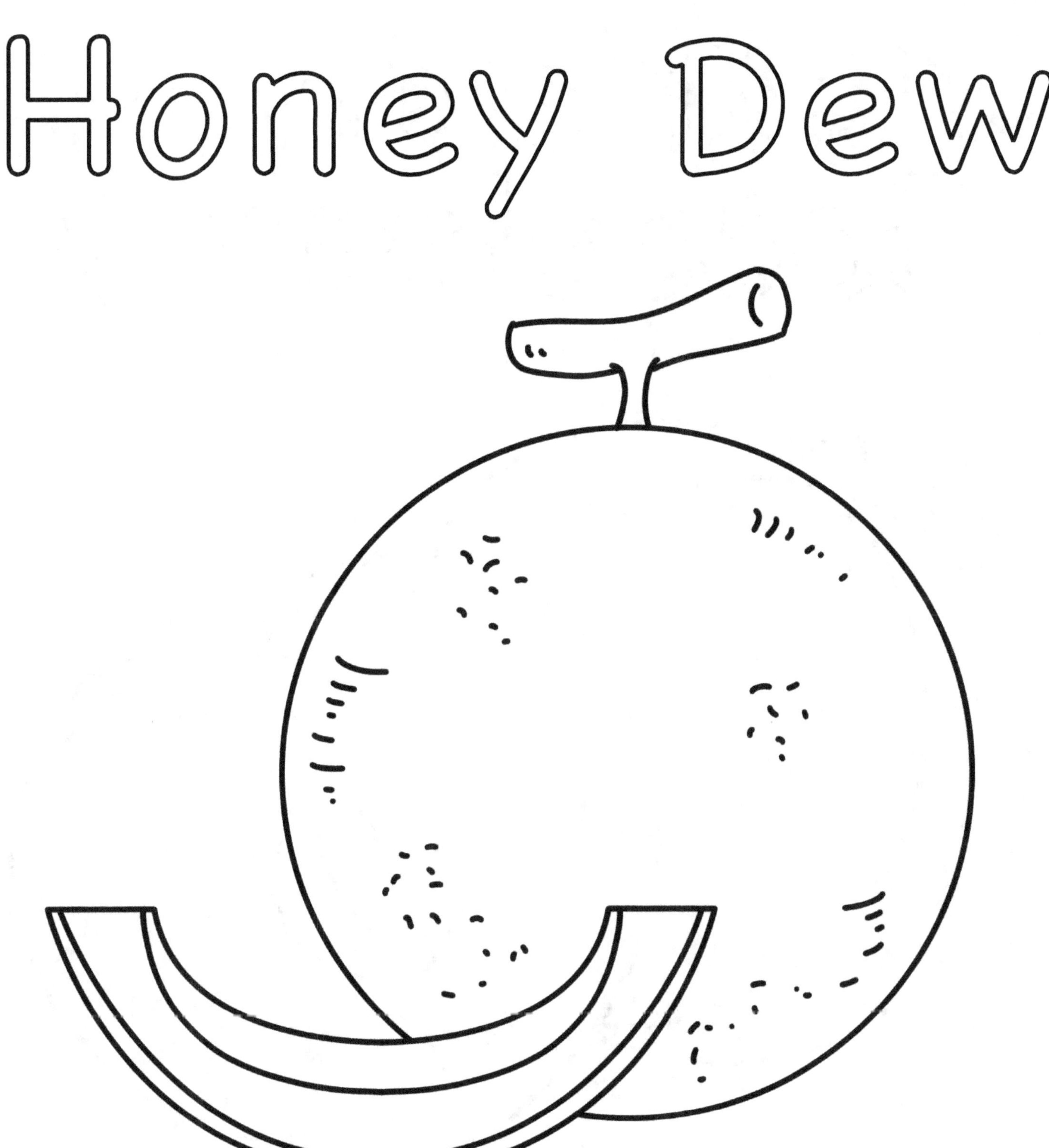

Honeydew has smooth, yellow or white skin.
The flesh of the fruit is green or pale green.
It is an oval-shaped fruit.

Indian Gooseberry

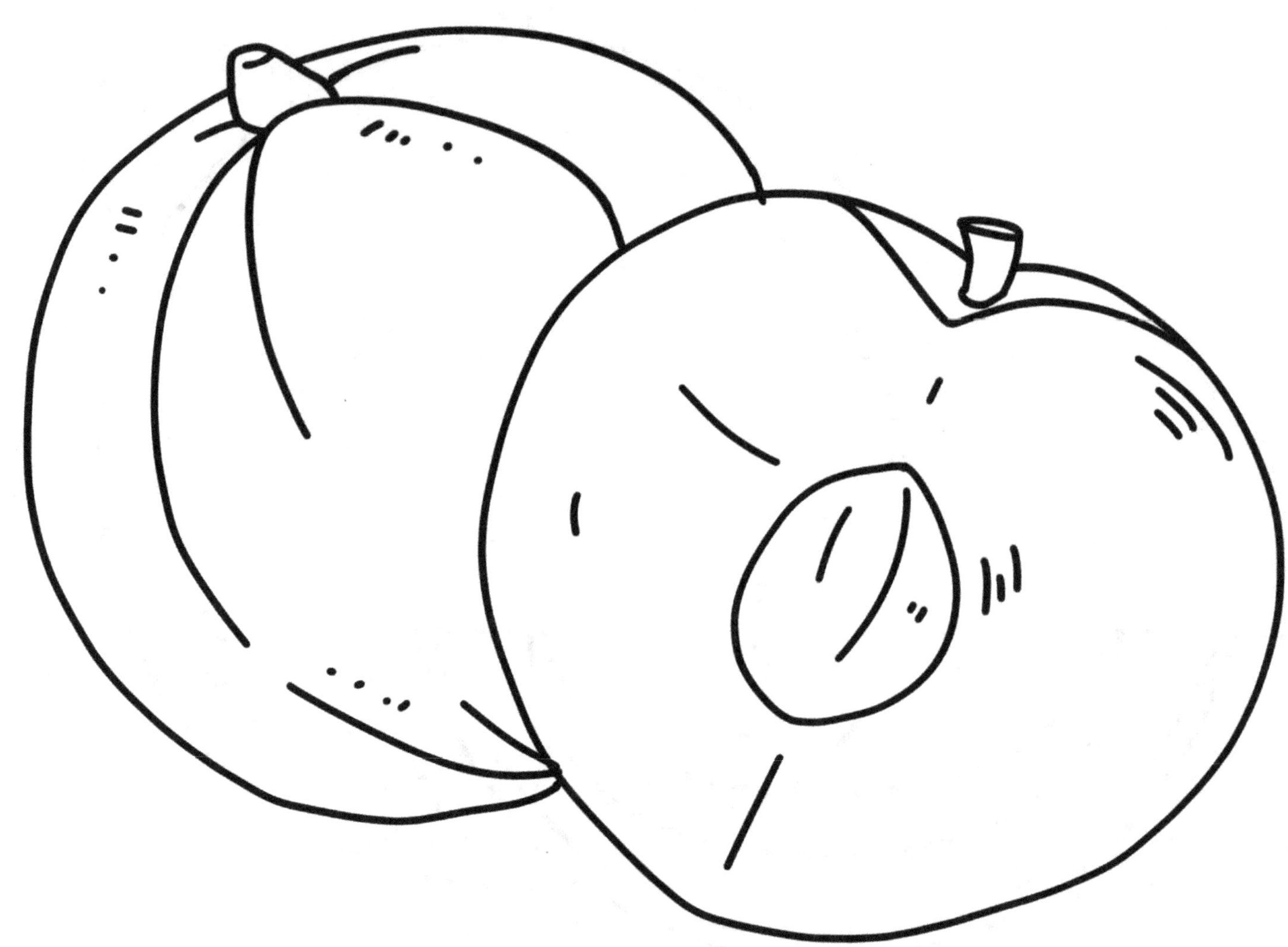

Commonly called "Amla", Indian Gooseberry is native to Nepal and India. It has many health benefits, especially in children.

Jackfruit

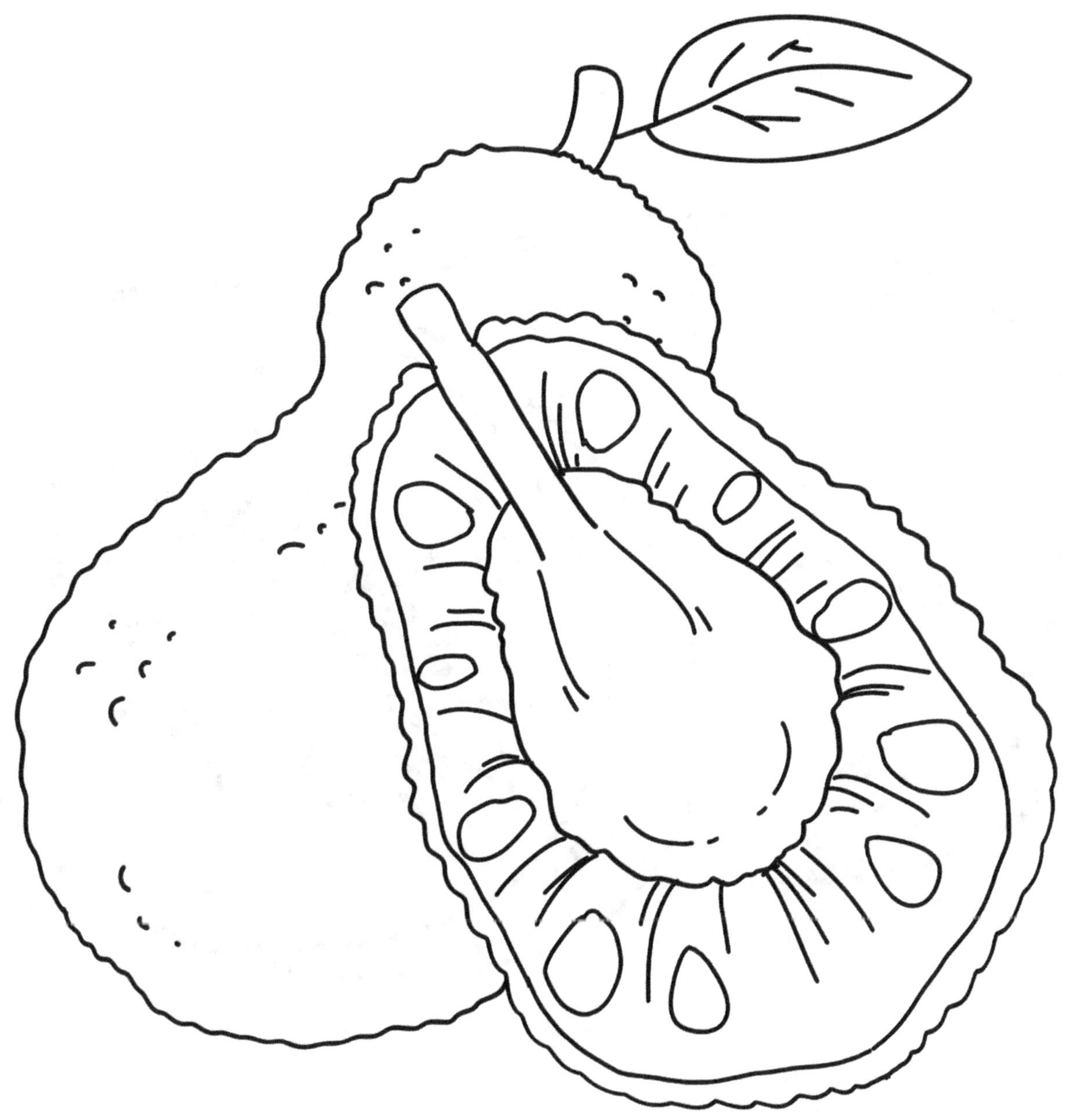

A jackfruit is multiple fruits, meaning
it is composed of hundreds of individual flowers,
and the fleshy petals of the flowers are consumed.

Kiwi

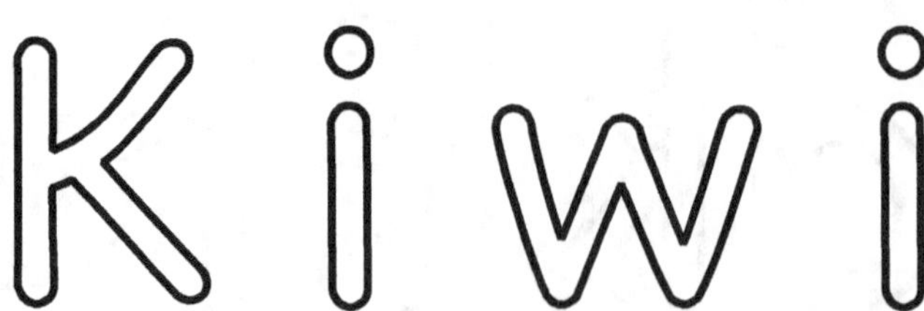

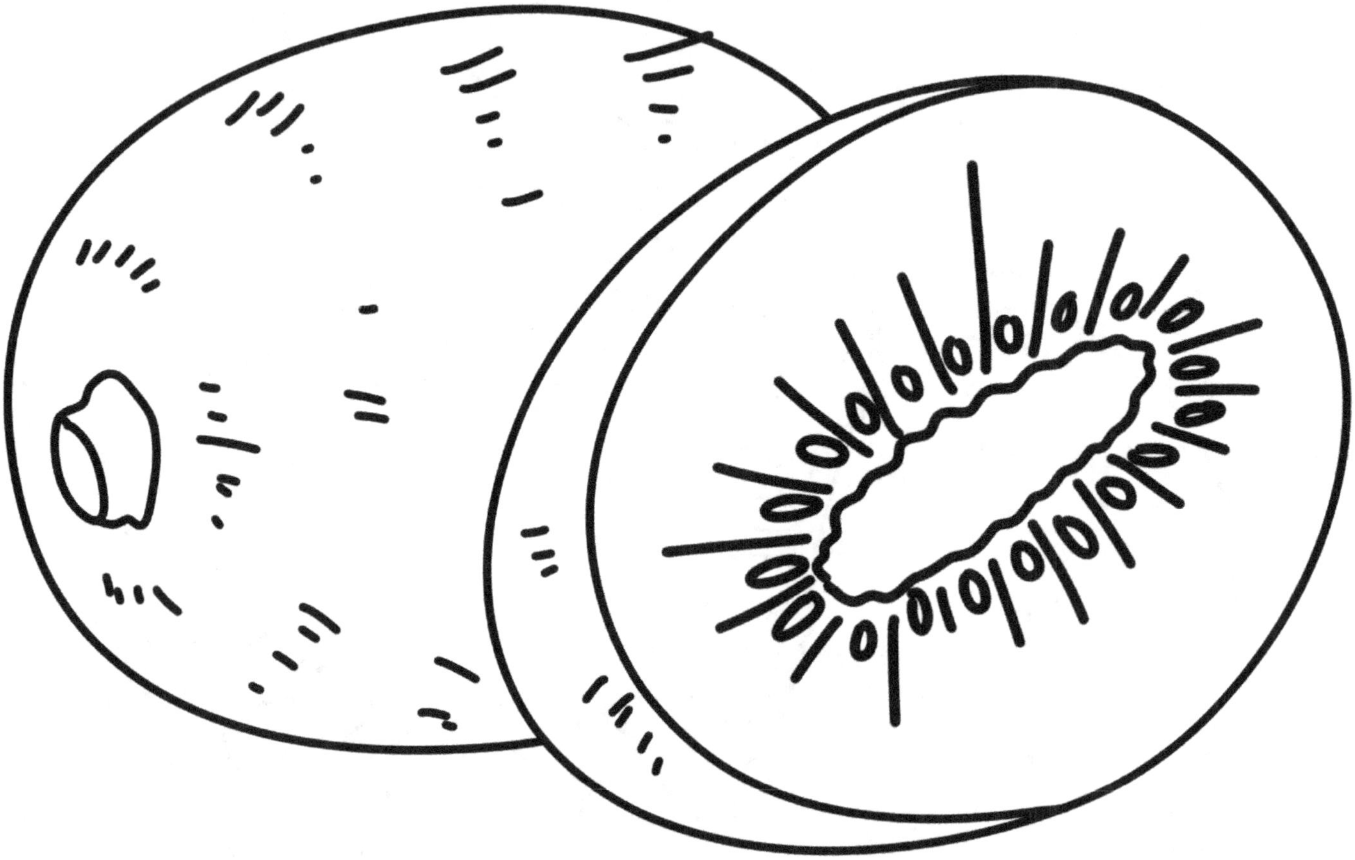

Kiwis are rich in vitamin C and antioxidants. They are good for the immune system of children. It has high fibre content. This fruit is good for heart health, digestive health, and helps building stronger immunity.

Lichi

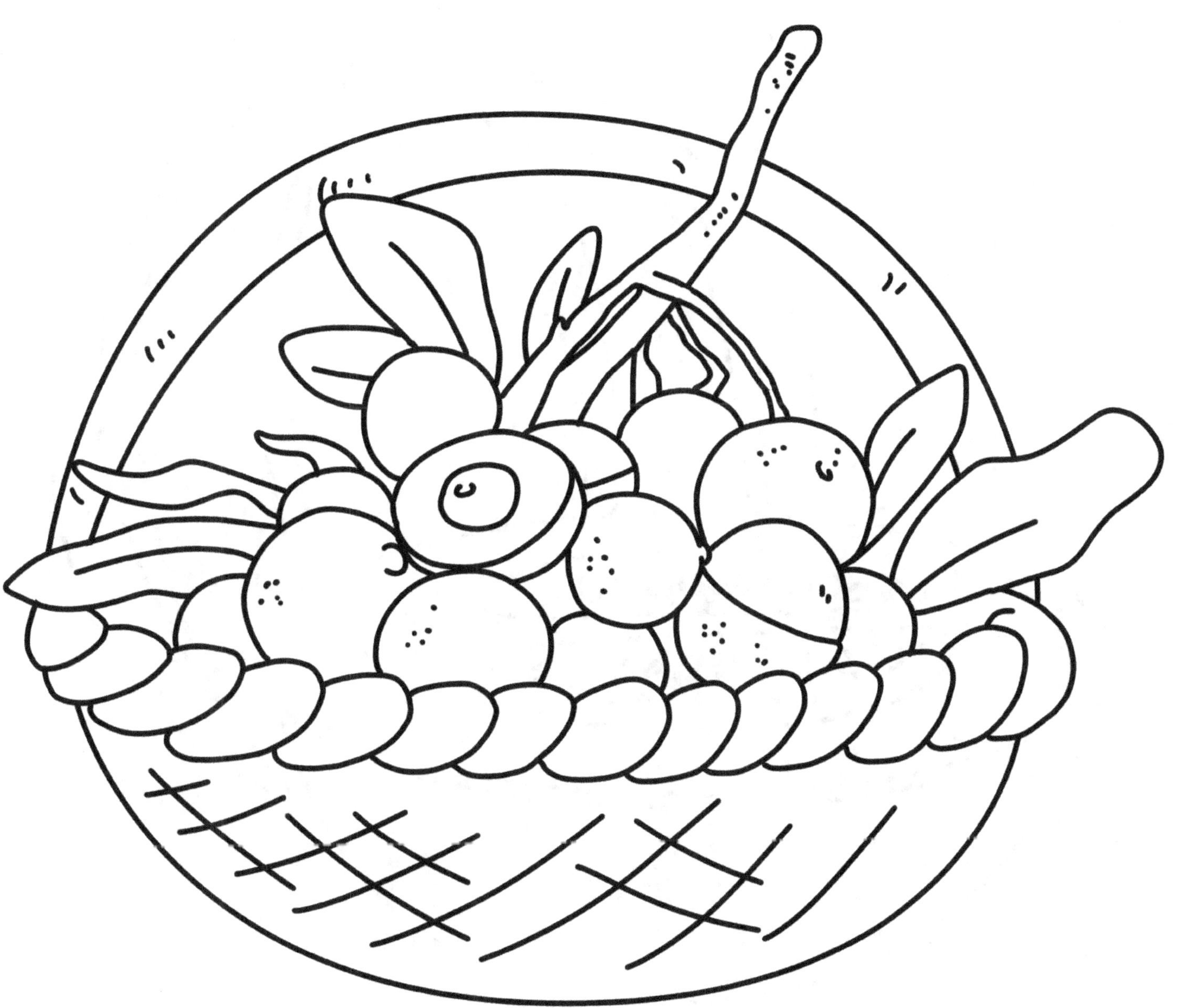

The inside of the fruit is pinkish-white in colour. It has a hard-spiky shell covering. The brown seed inside the fruit is also rigid and should not be eaten.

Muskmelon

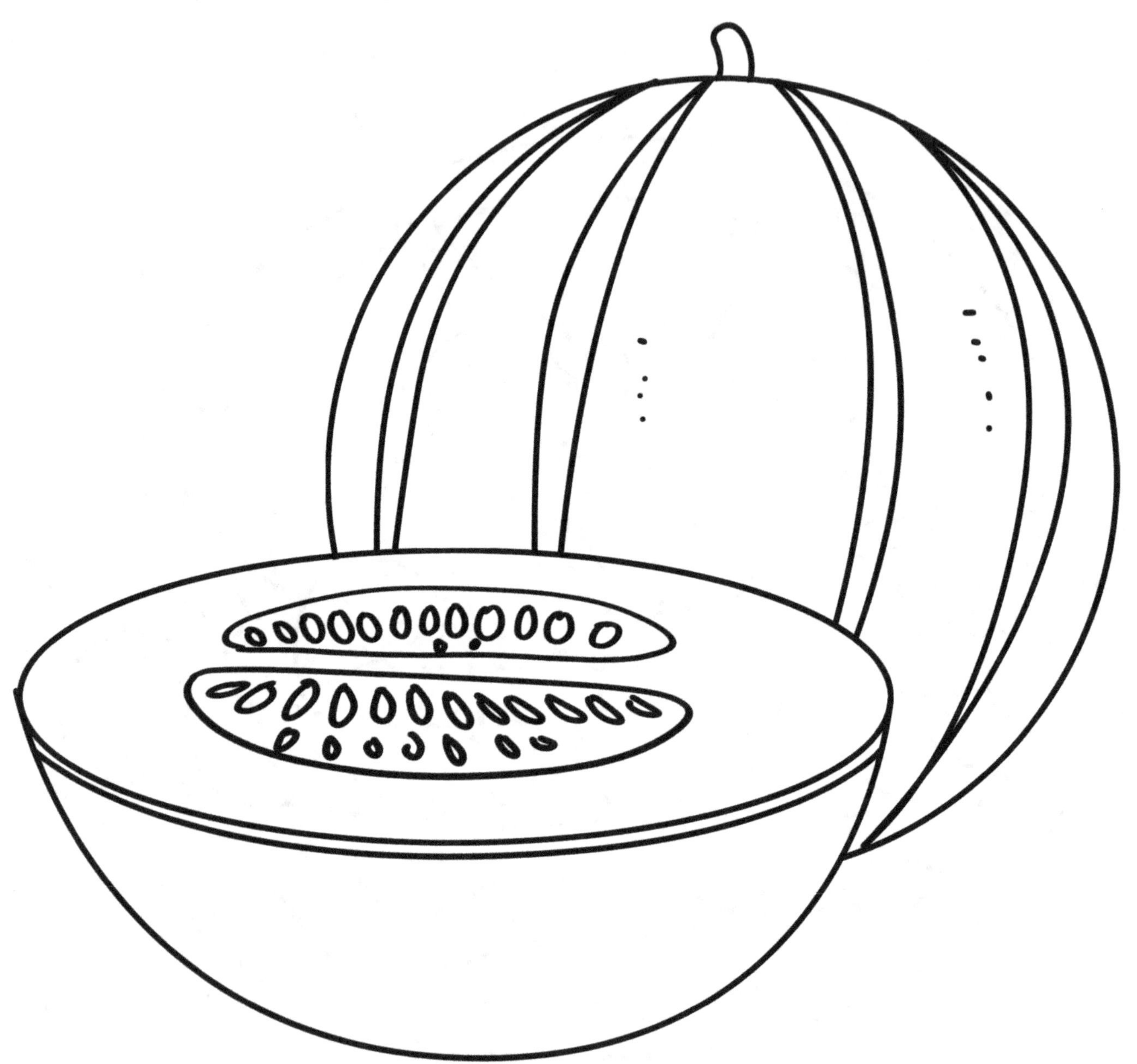

Muskmelons are a type of melon. The name comes from the words "musk", meaning "perfume" in Persian and "melon", meaning "apple-shaped melon" in Latin.

Nappa Cabbage

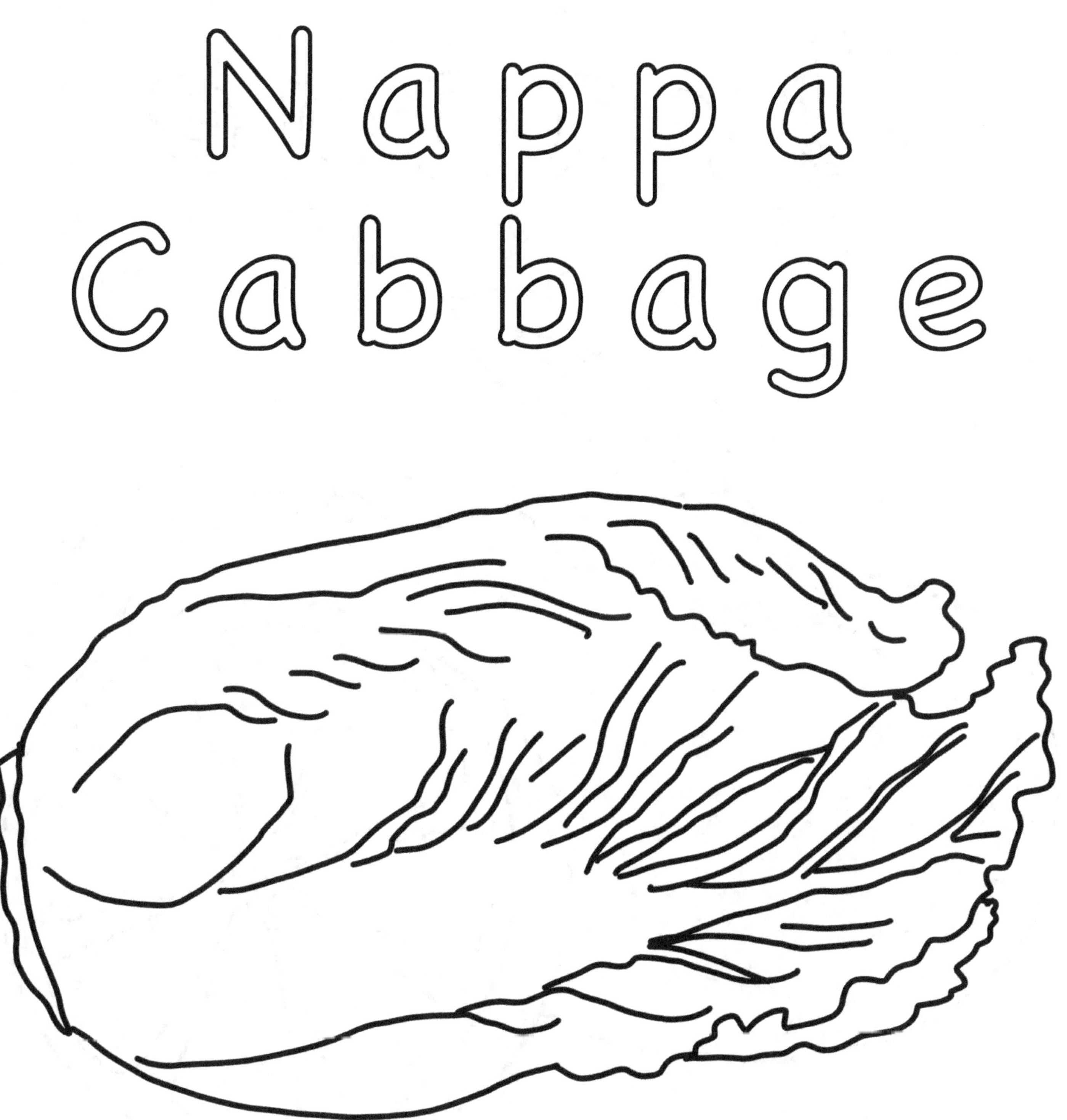

Napa cabbages have succulent stems
and ruffled leaves. They have an oblong shape and
have both a tender and crisp texture.

Orange

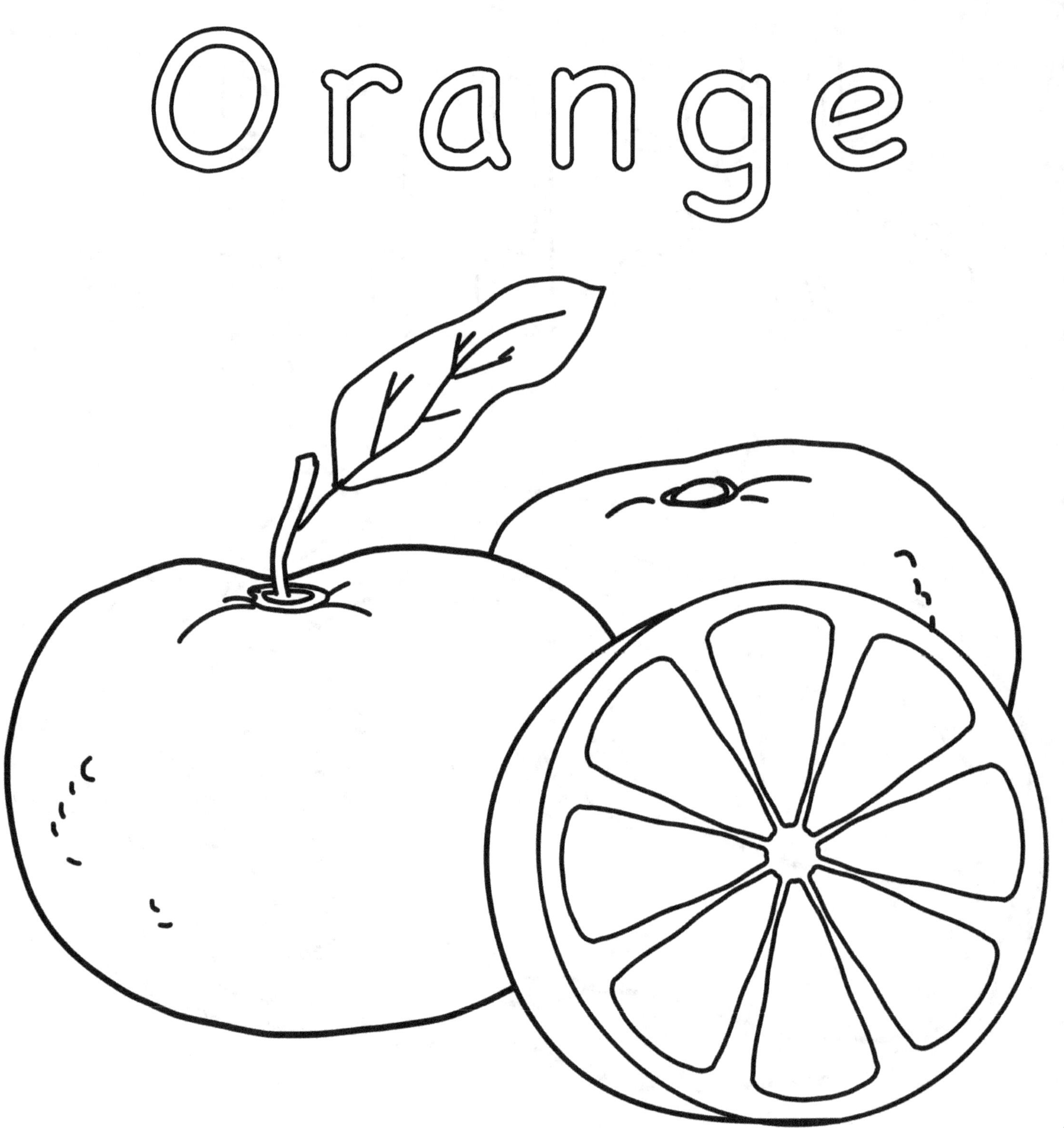

Oranges are orange-coloured round fruits.
They have dark-green shiny leaves. These are citrus fruits, which
mean they are rich in Vitamin C.

Papaya

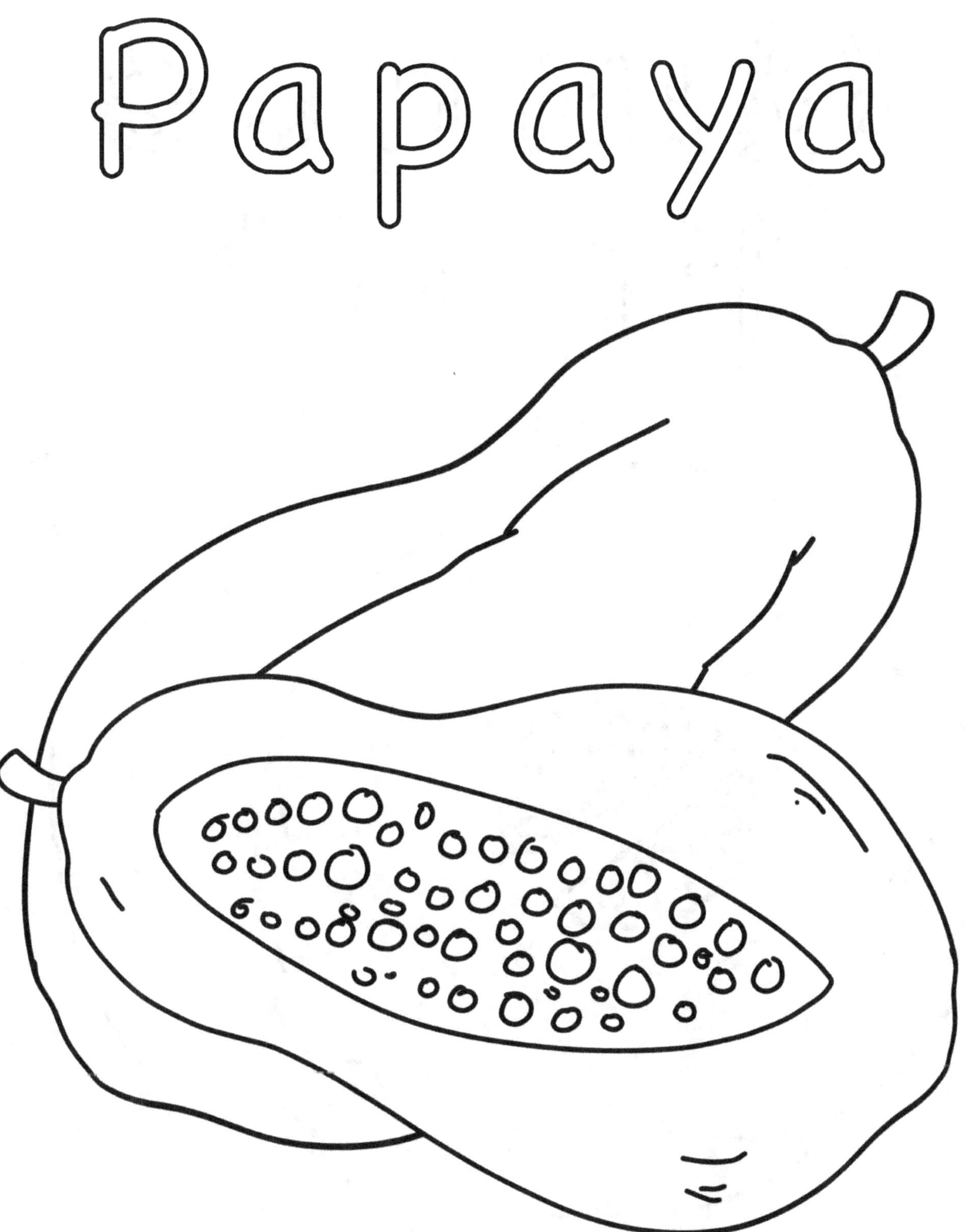

Papayas are native to America's tropical region.
They need a warm climate to grow.
Papayas are rich in calcium and iron.

Quince Fruit

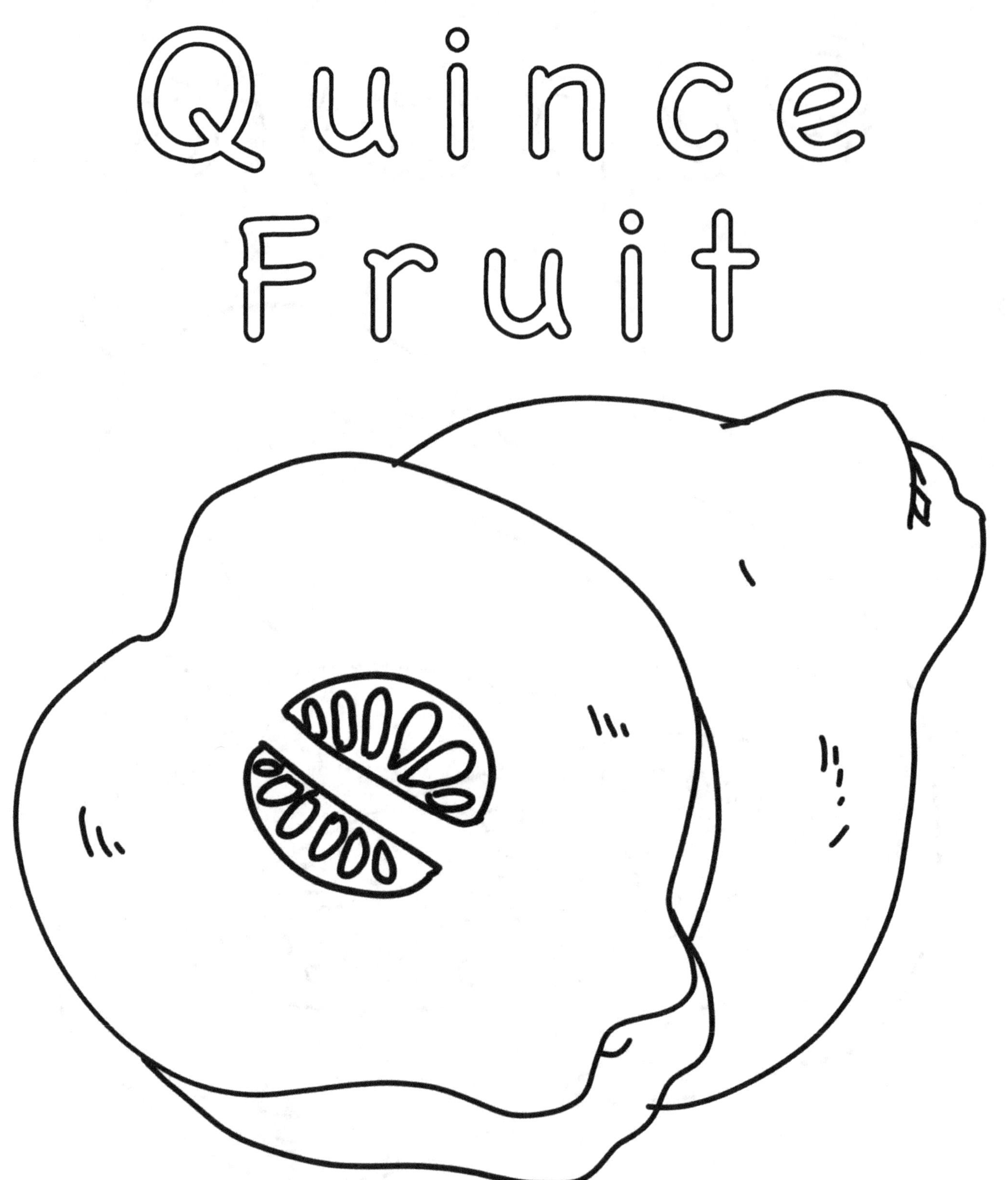

Quince fruit grows on small trees. Quince belongs to the same family as apples or pears. They are green in colour when unripe and turn golden-yellow when ripe.

Rose Apple

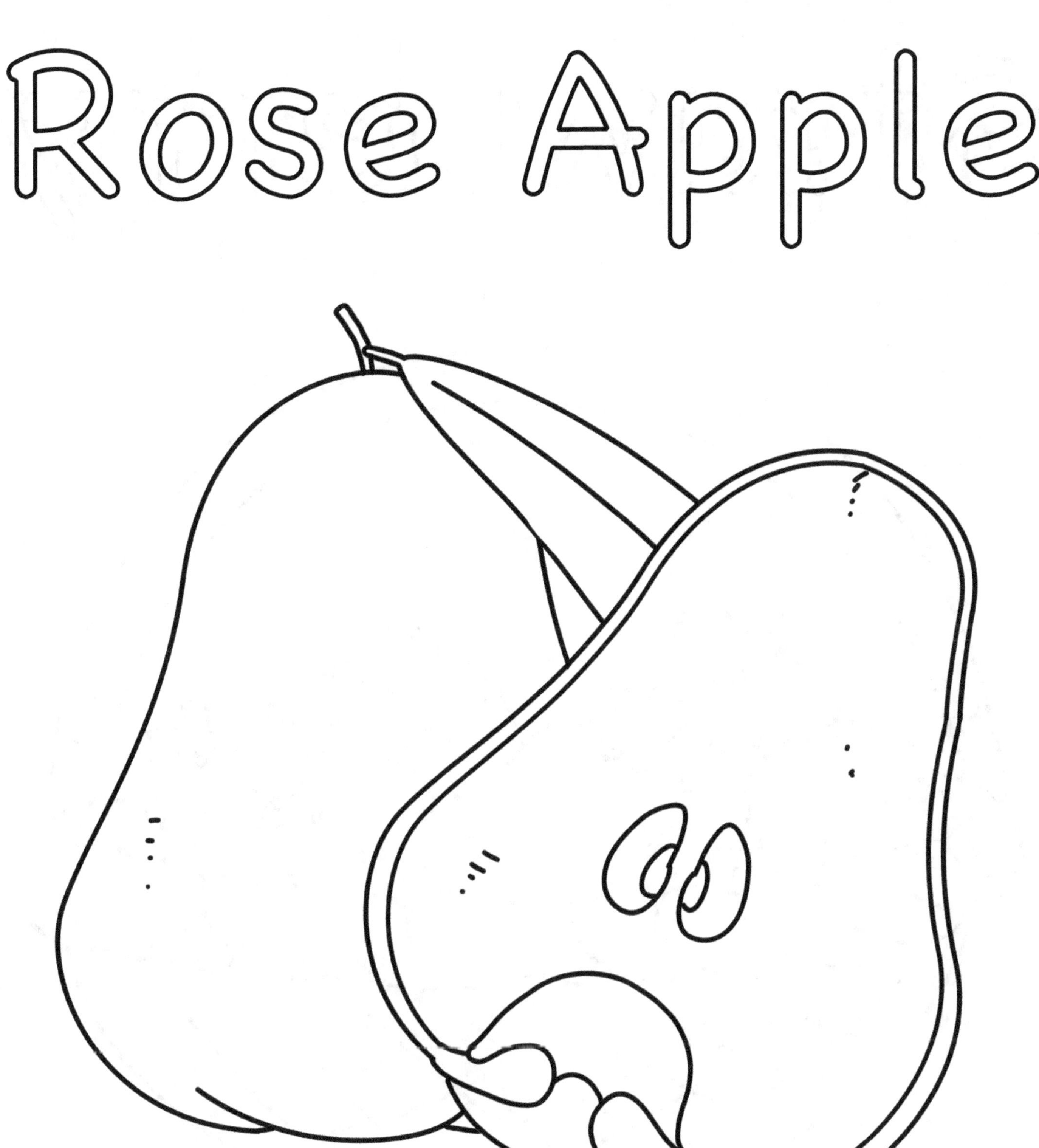

Rose apple is rich in fibre content. These are hence, very helpful to protect against digestive troubles. These also help in regulating blood sugar.

Strawberry

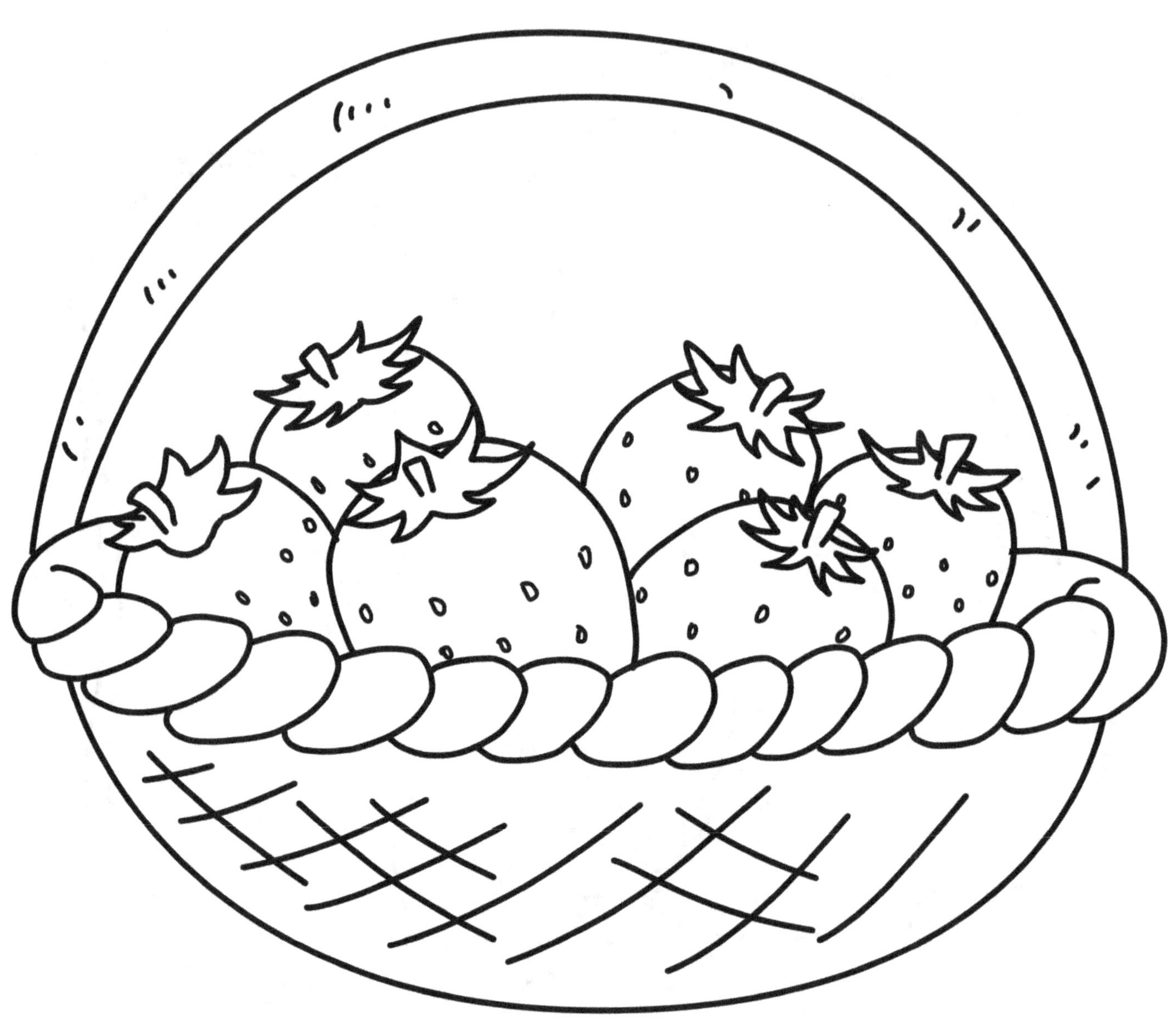

Strawberry is among the healthiest fruits for kids. It's juicy and sweet. Strawberries have a striking, attractive appearance.

Tamarind

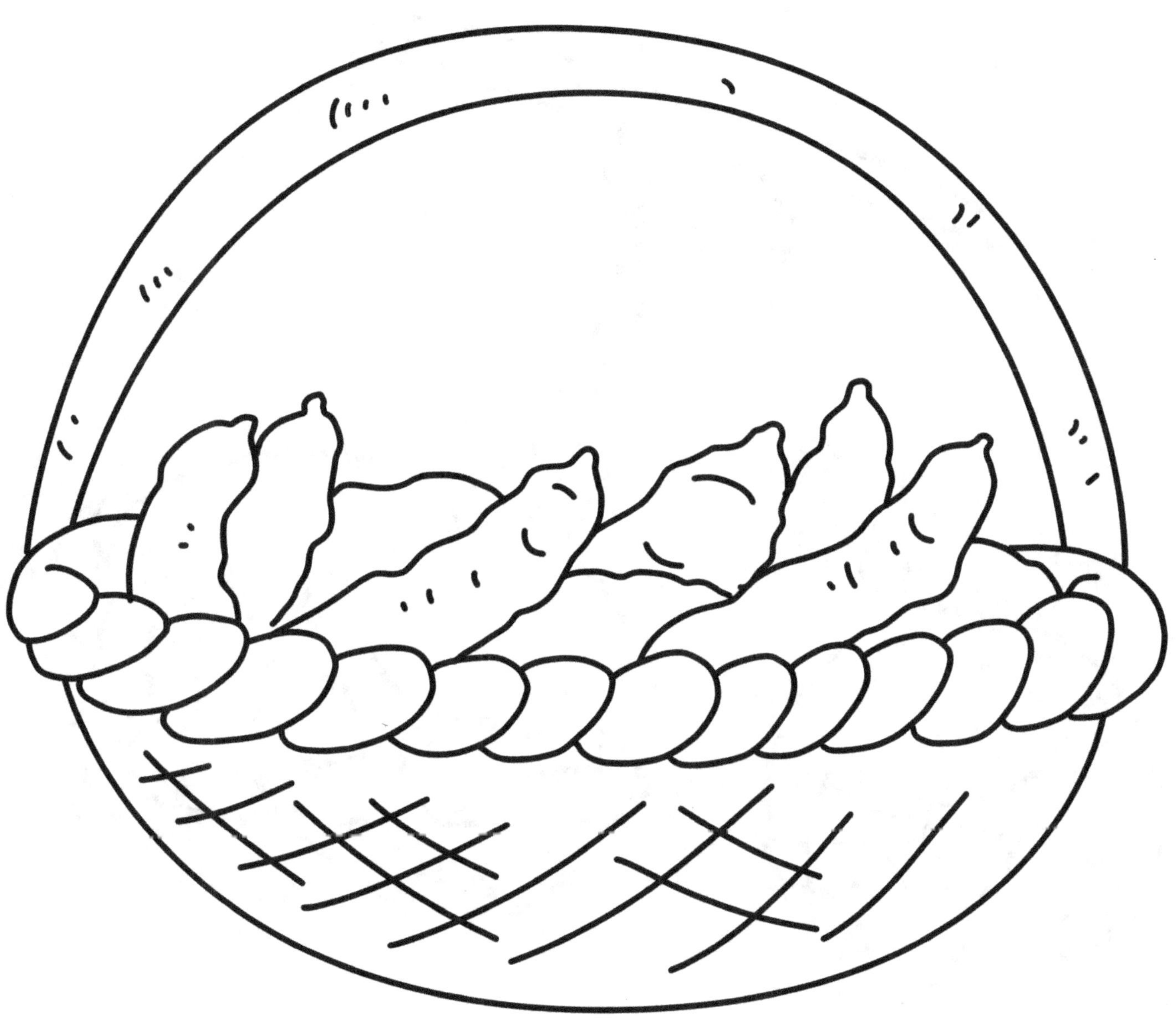

The pulp of young tamarind is sour and green in colour. It becomes juicy pulp when it ripens. It changes to paste-like in texture and become more sweet-sour.

Ugni

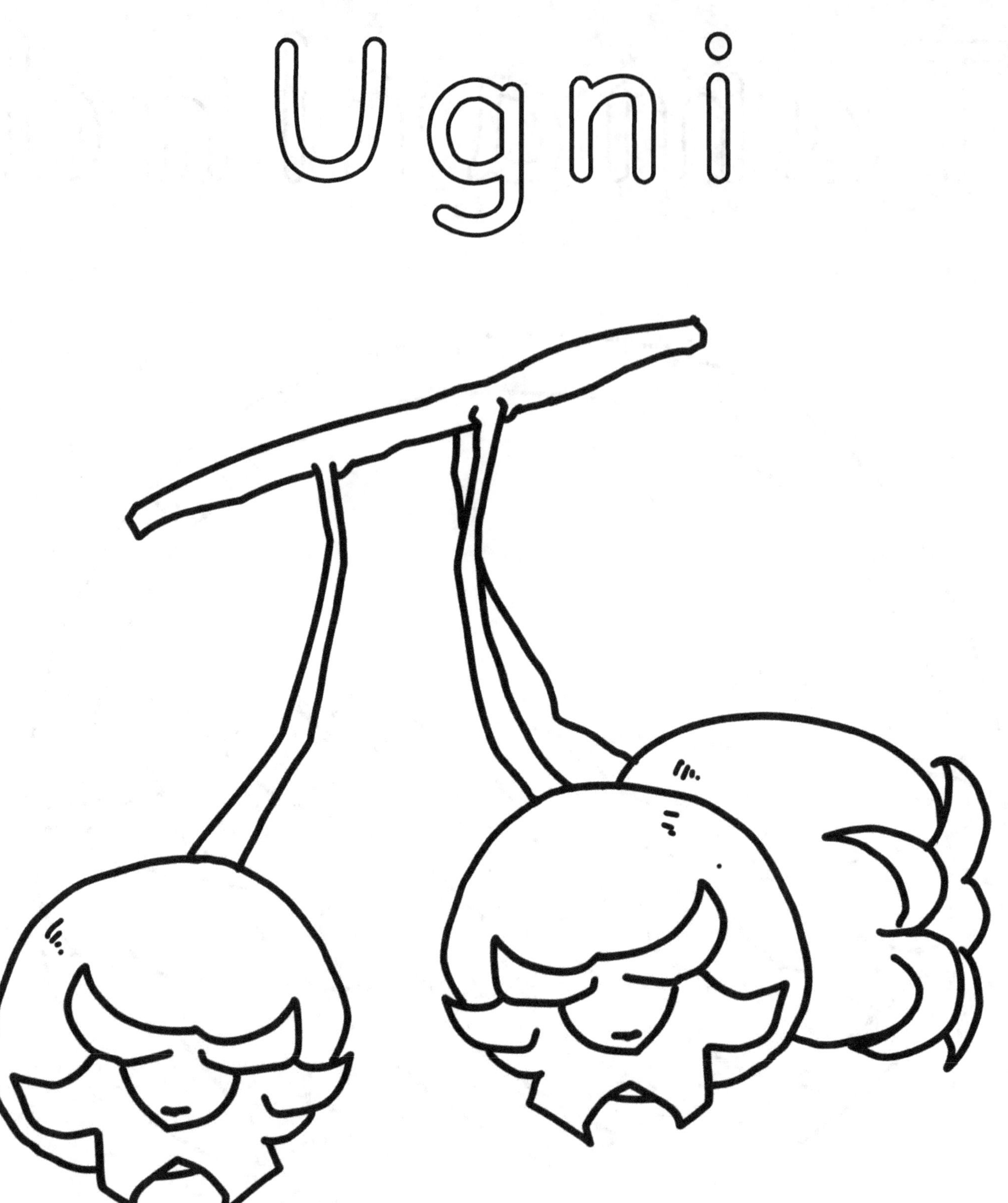

Ugnis are small evergreen shrubs.
This fruit is a small purple or red berry in color.
The size is about 1 cm in diameter with multiple seeds.

Victorian Plum

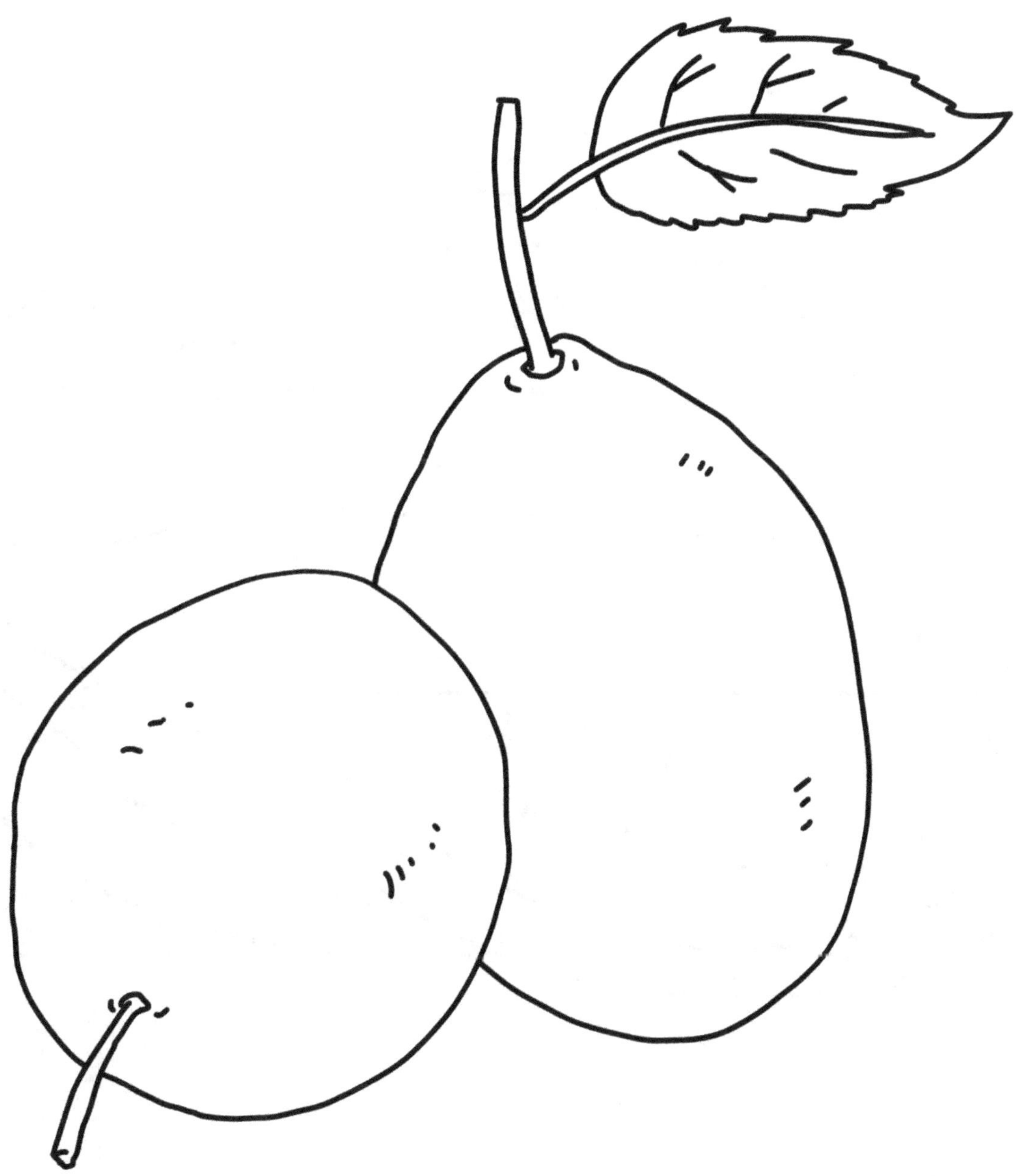

A Victoria plum is a sweet fruit. It grows on the plum tree.
It is called a prune when it is dried.
It has a slight taste of almond.

Watermelon

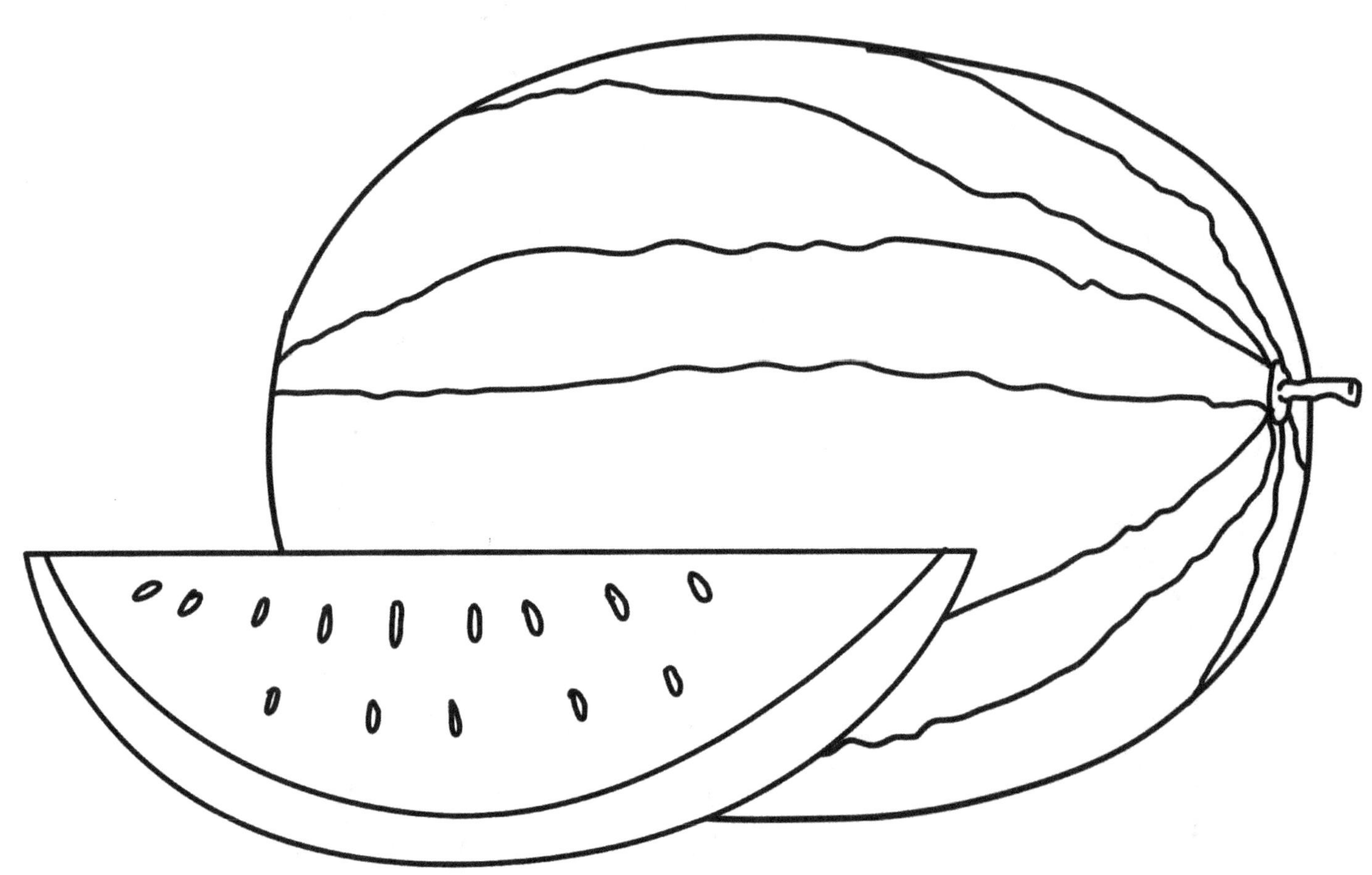

Watermelon is both a fruit as well as a vegetable.
It has 92% water content, and hence the name.
Its origin is in West Africa.

Ximenia

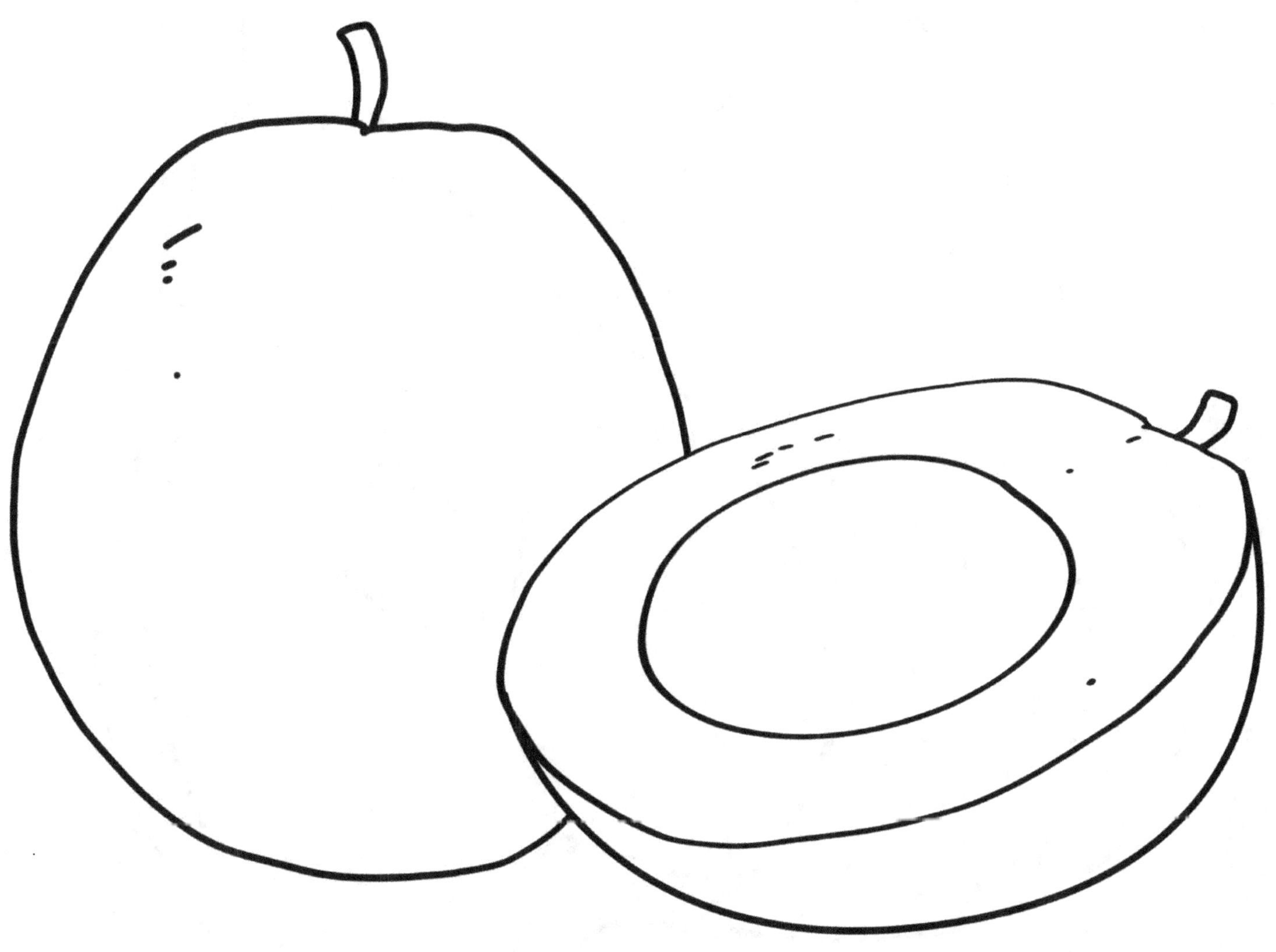

This fruit has a unique flavour.
The flavour can range from bitter to very sweet, depending on the fruit. The fruit has a sticky texture.

Yali Asian Pear

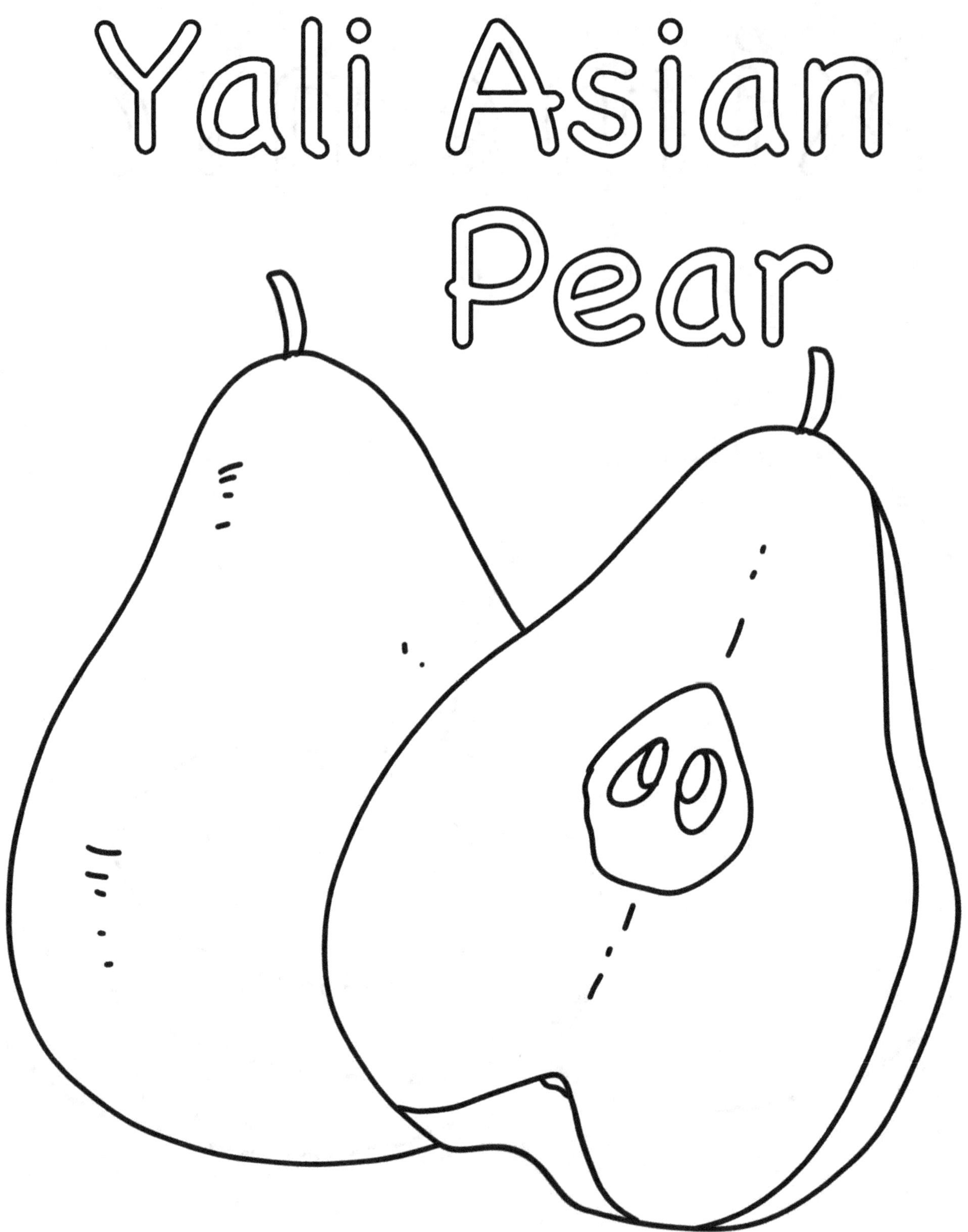

Originated in Japan, Yali Asian Pear has yellow, brown and yellowish-brown skin. The ones that originated in China have greenish-yellow skin.

Zucchini

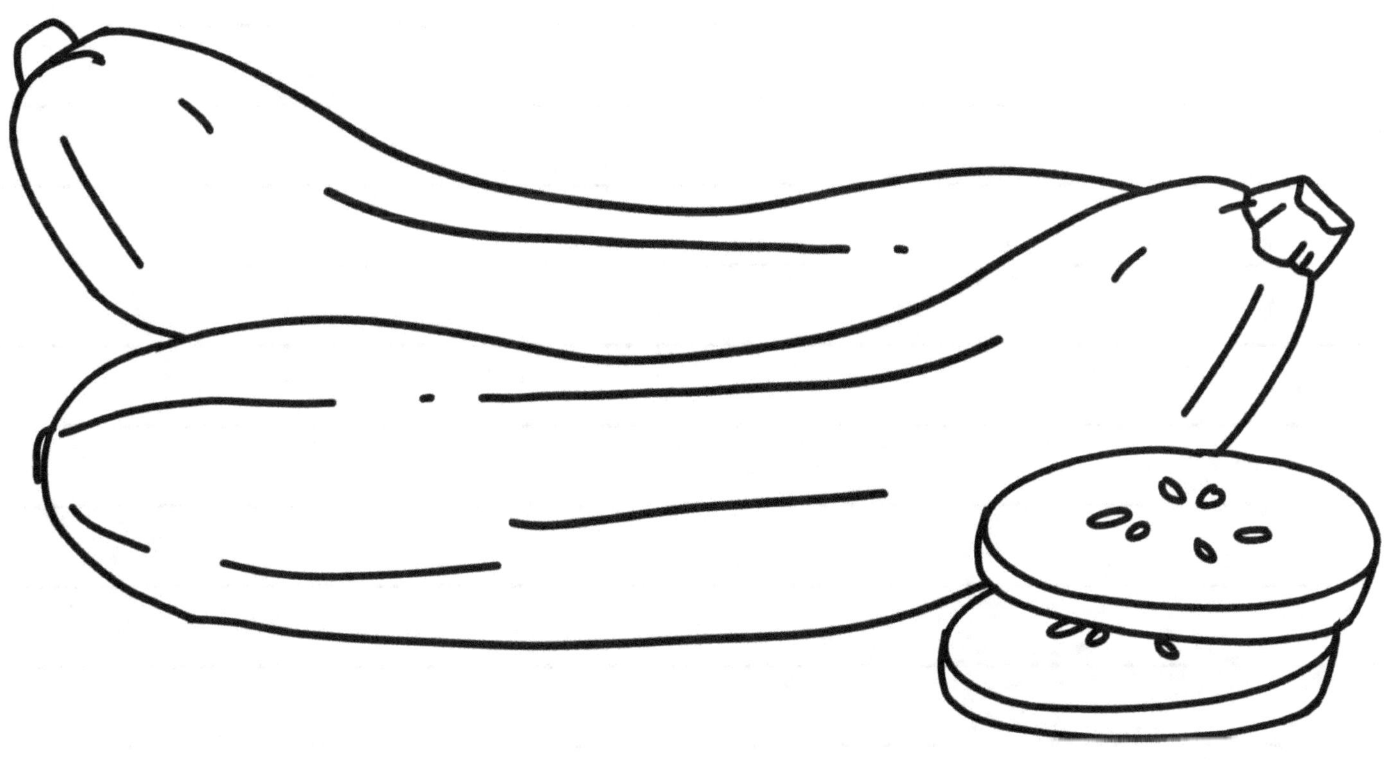

Zucchini is also called courgette in some
parts of the world. The fruit has soft, thin skin.
It's sausage-shaped and has rounded ends.

Name your favorite fruit or vegetable and write a few lines about it

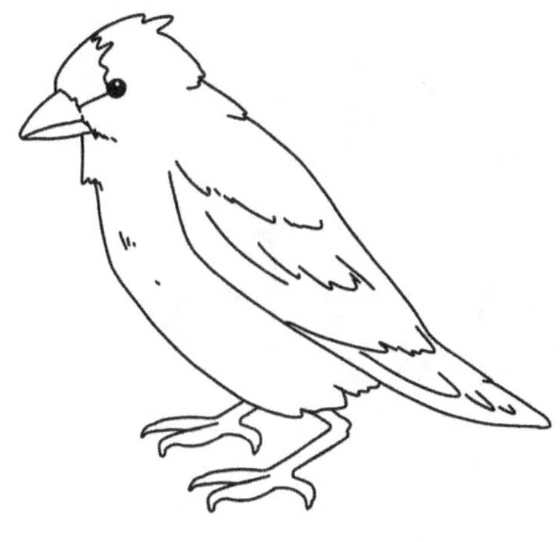

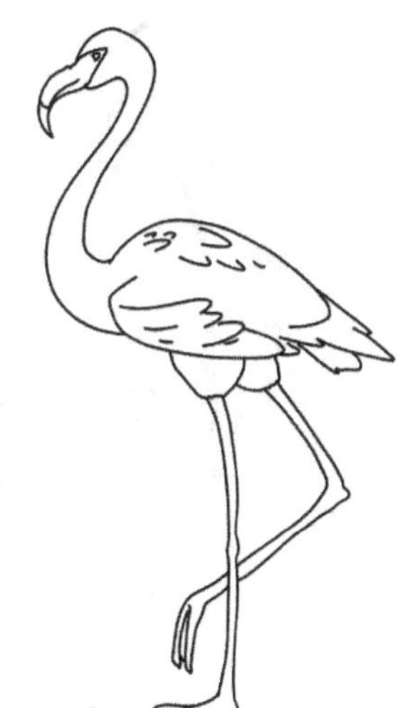

BIRDS

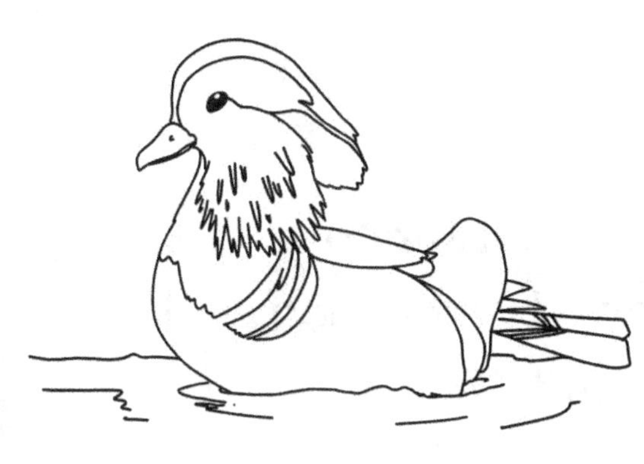

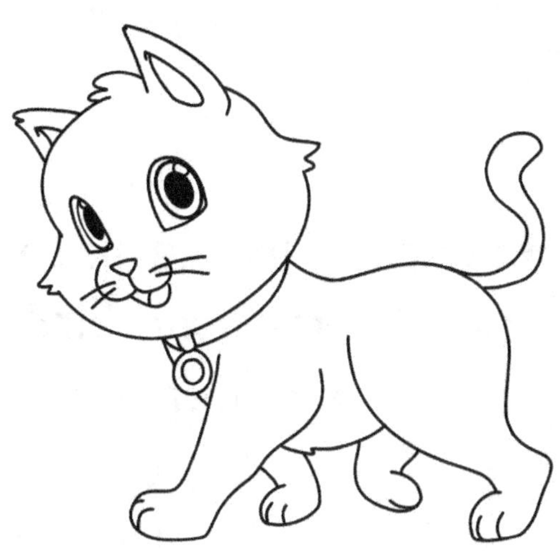

American Goldfinch

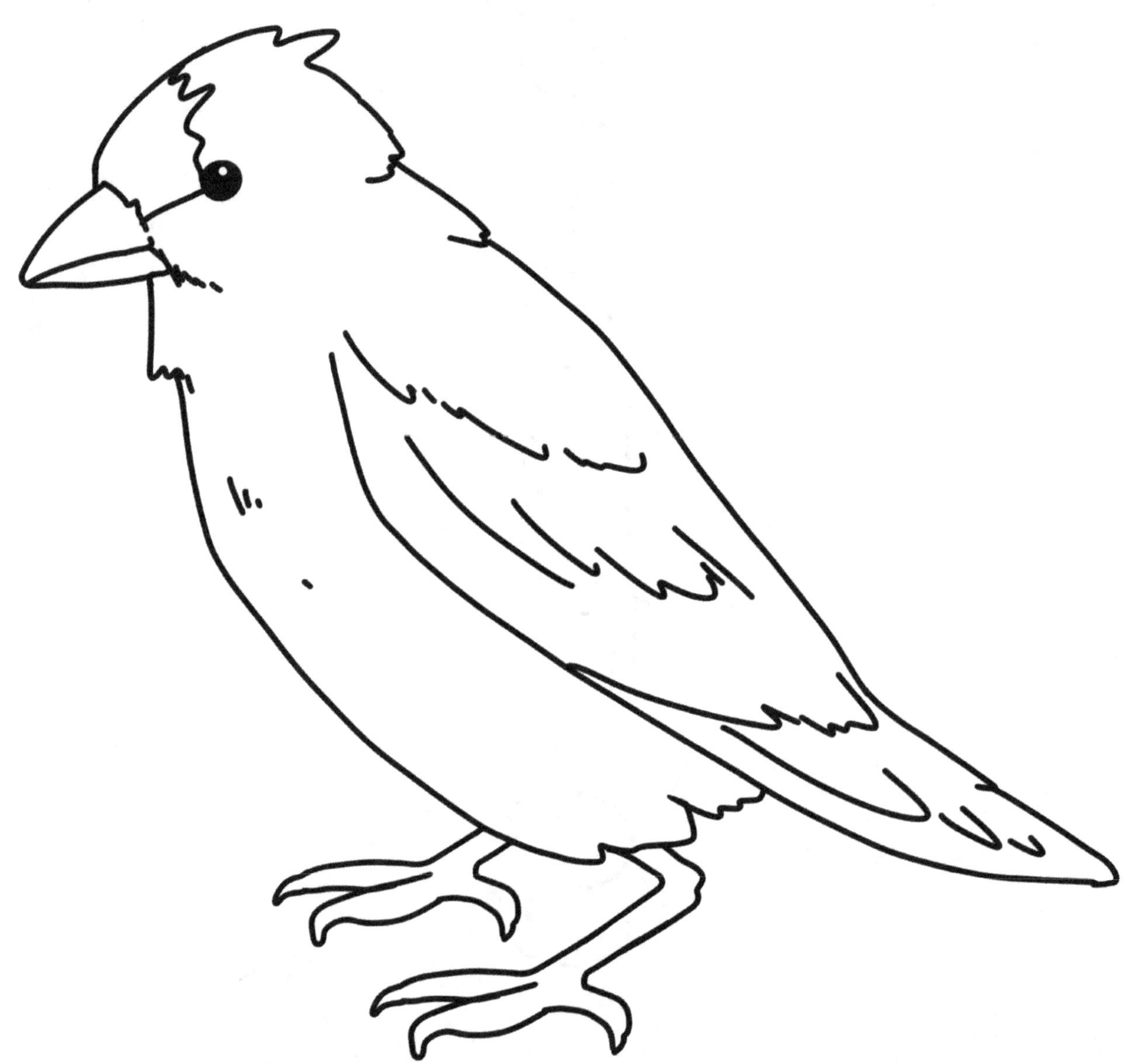

Belonging to the finch family, an American Goldfinch is a small North American bird. These birds are pretty common in the winter in Western Washington and Oregon.

Crow

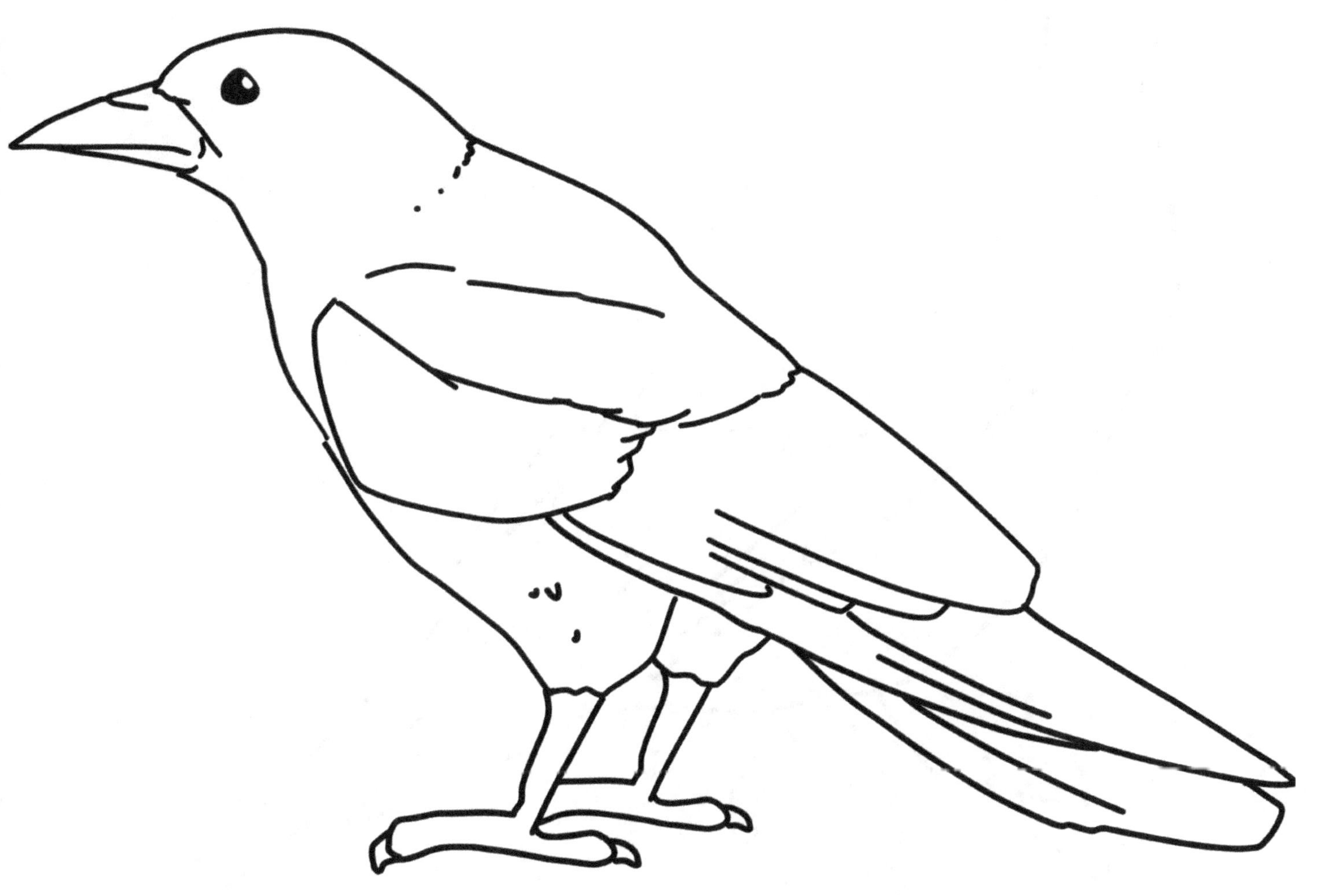

Crows have black feathers.
Their feathers usually look shining because of
their deep colour. They make a loud "Caw" sound.

Eastern Bluebird

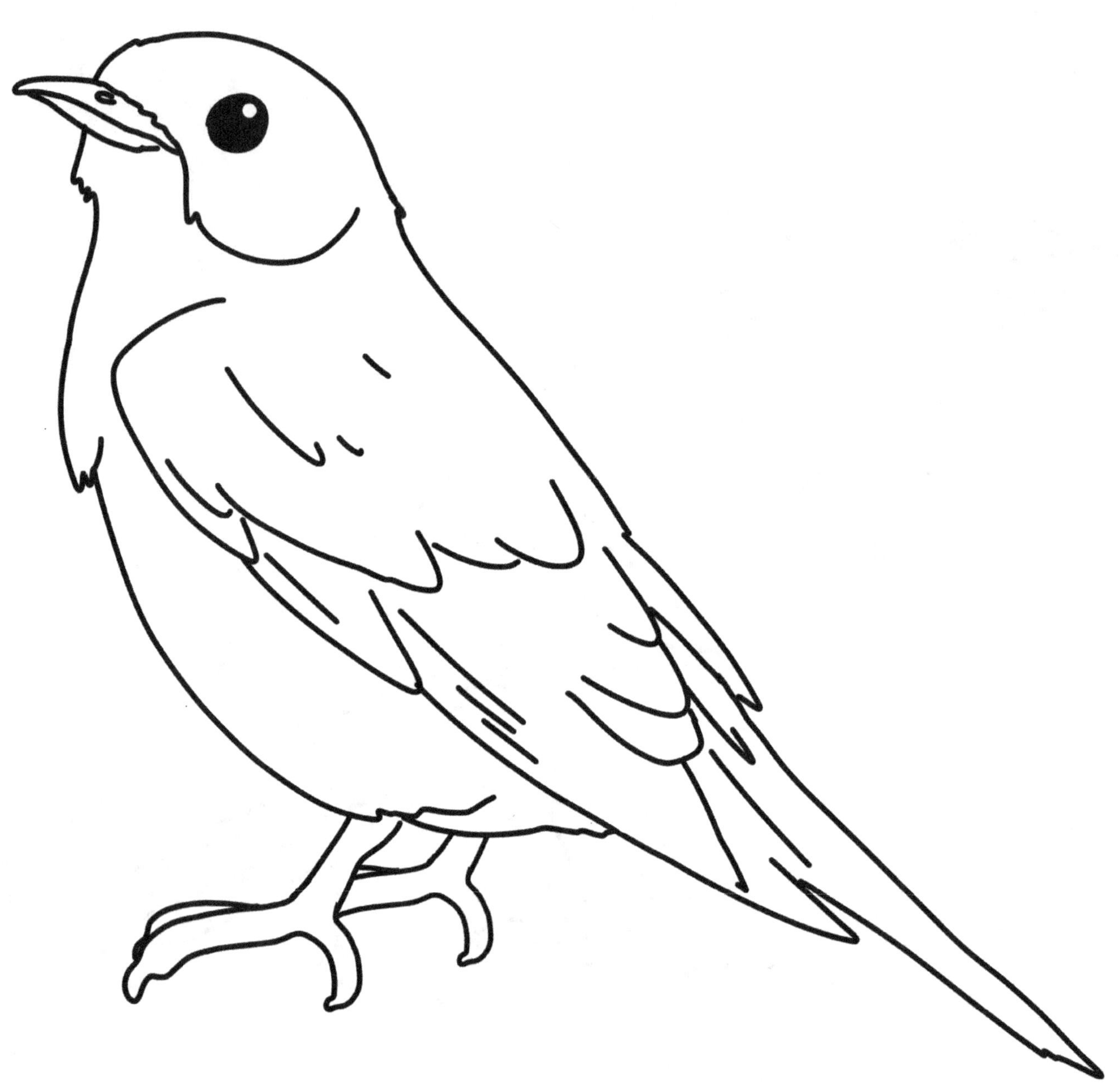

Male Eastern Bluebirds have bright-blue wings and head. The females are duller in colour and have greyish heads with blue wings.

Flamingo

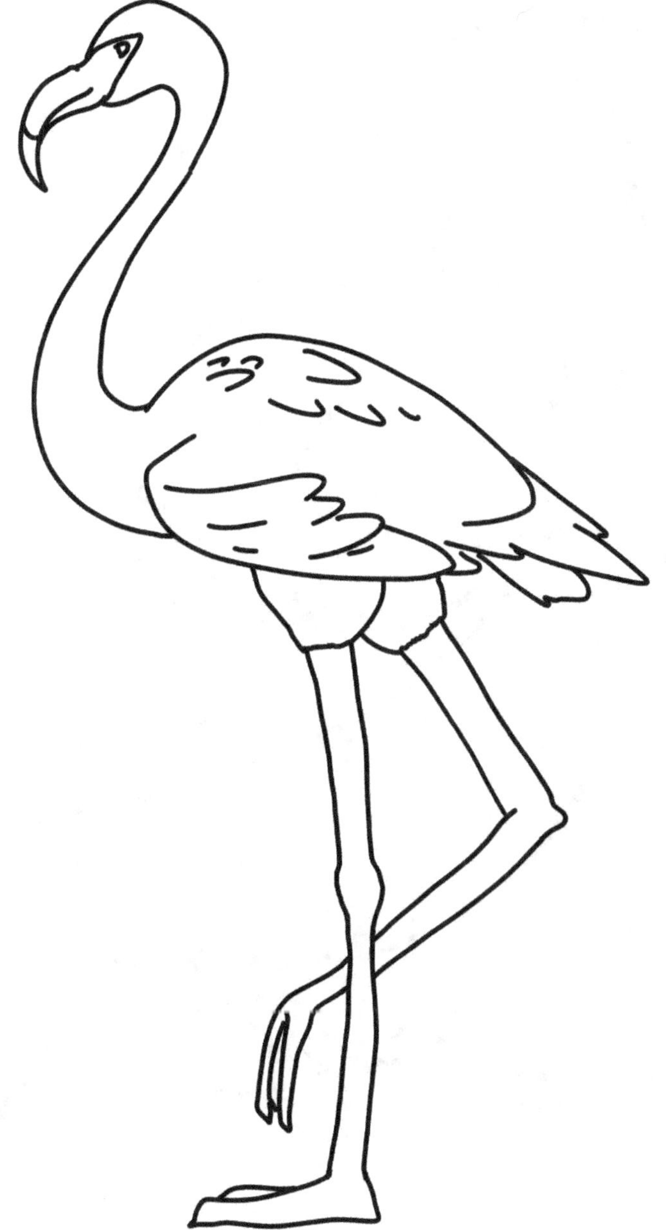

Flamingos have long legs and curving beaks.
They are bright orange. People love to watch flamingoes in the
nature preserves and zoos.

House Sparrow

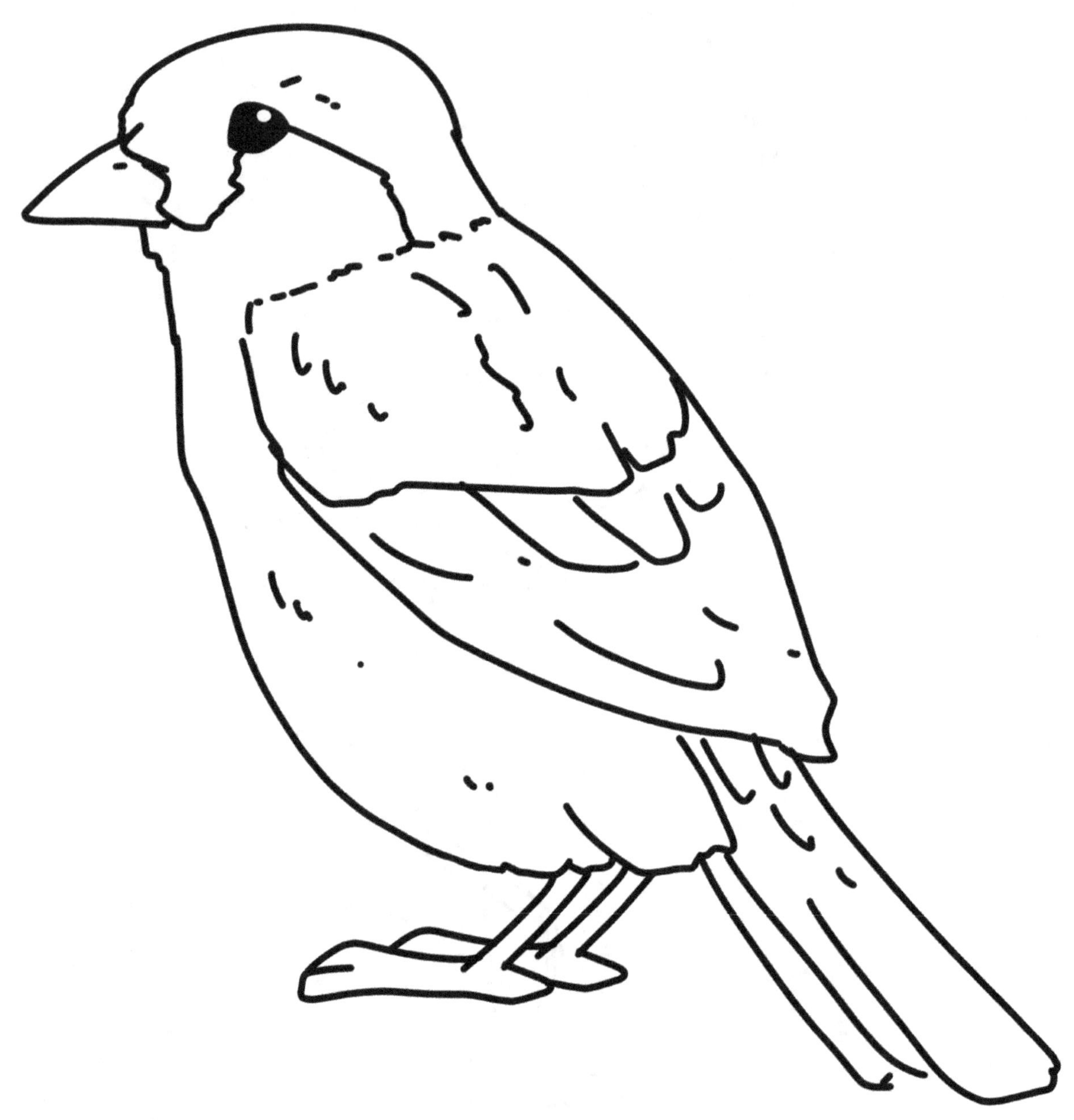

Sparrows eat seeds, insects, berries, moths,
and fruits and berries. They also feed their young babies
with insects to grow them strong.

Hen

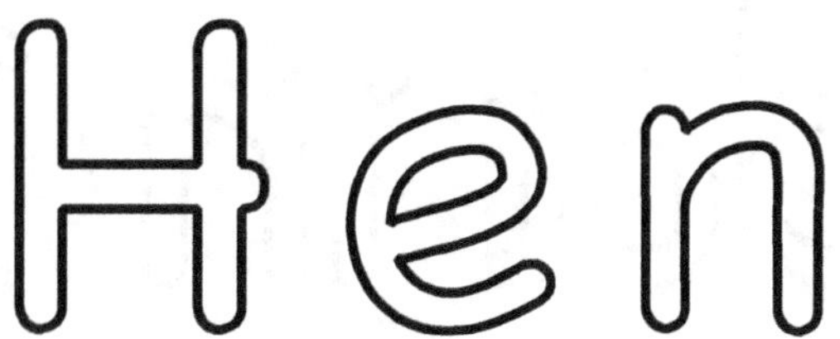

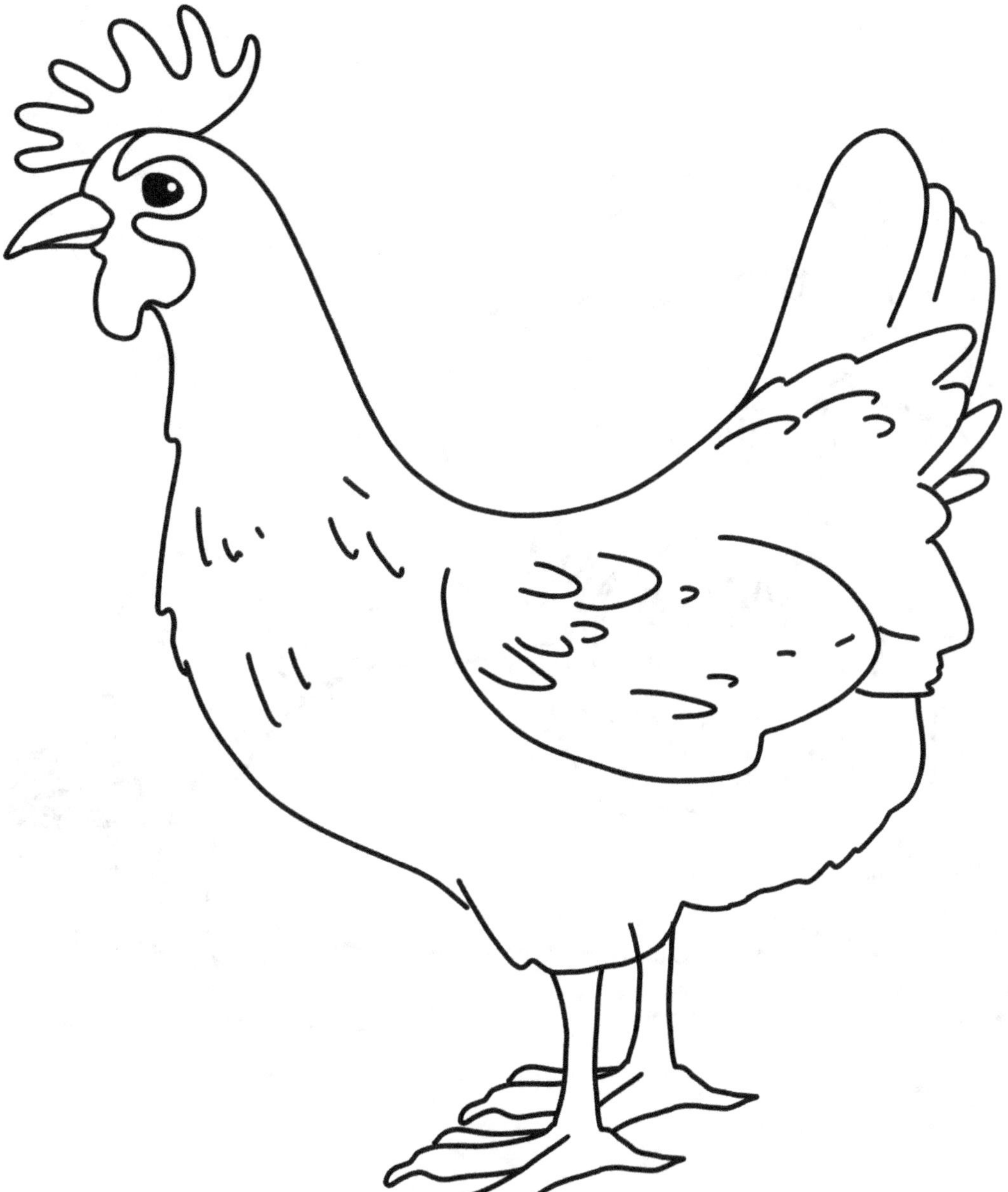

A female chicken is called a hen. Hens lay eggs.
The eggs then hatch into chicks. Hens are primarily
raised for egg production.

Mandarin Duck

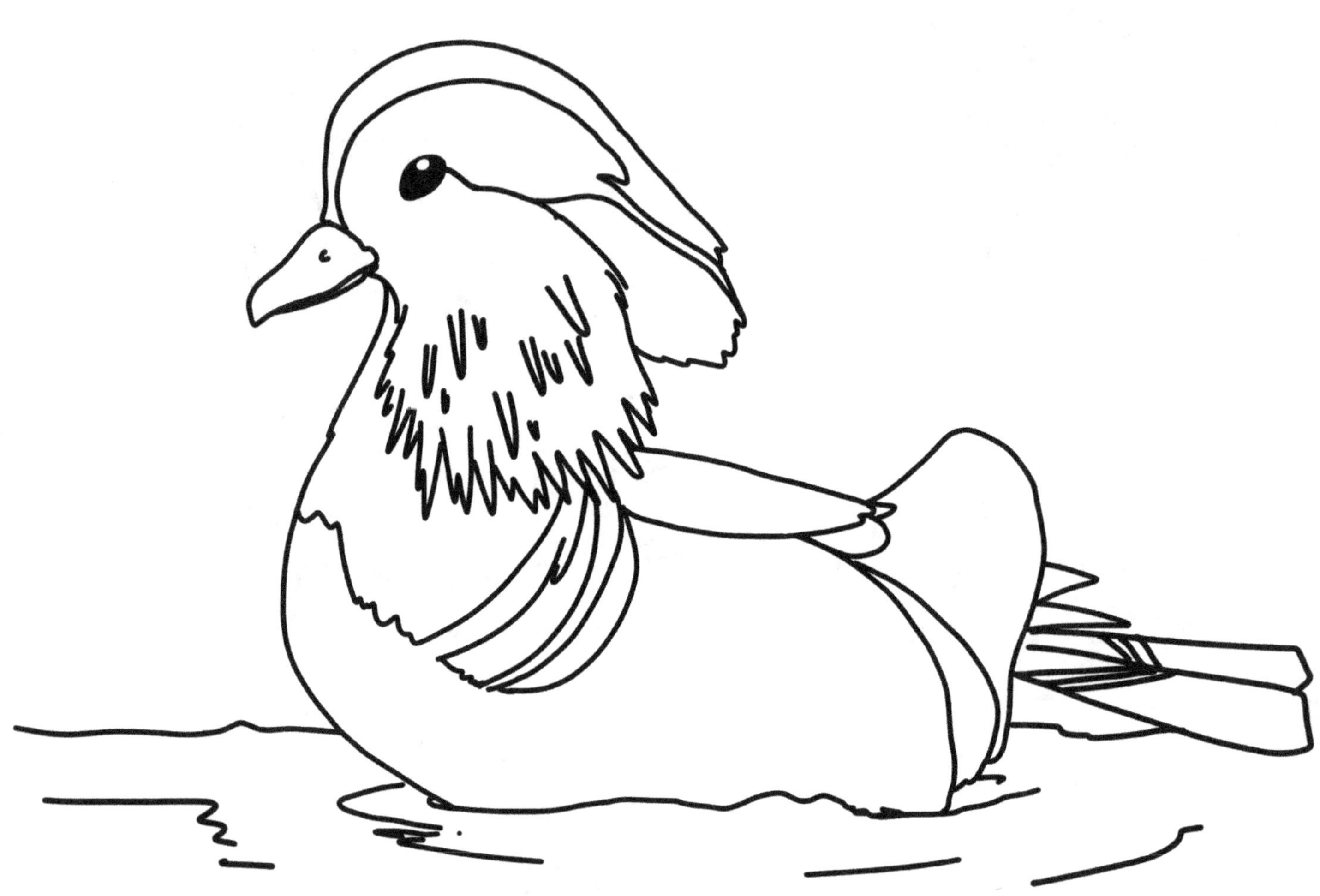

Both male and female mandarin ducks have crests.
However, the males have a more pronounced purple crest.
They also have bright yellow-orange or red beak.

Ostrich

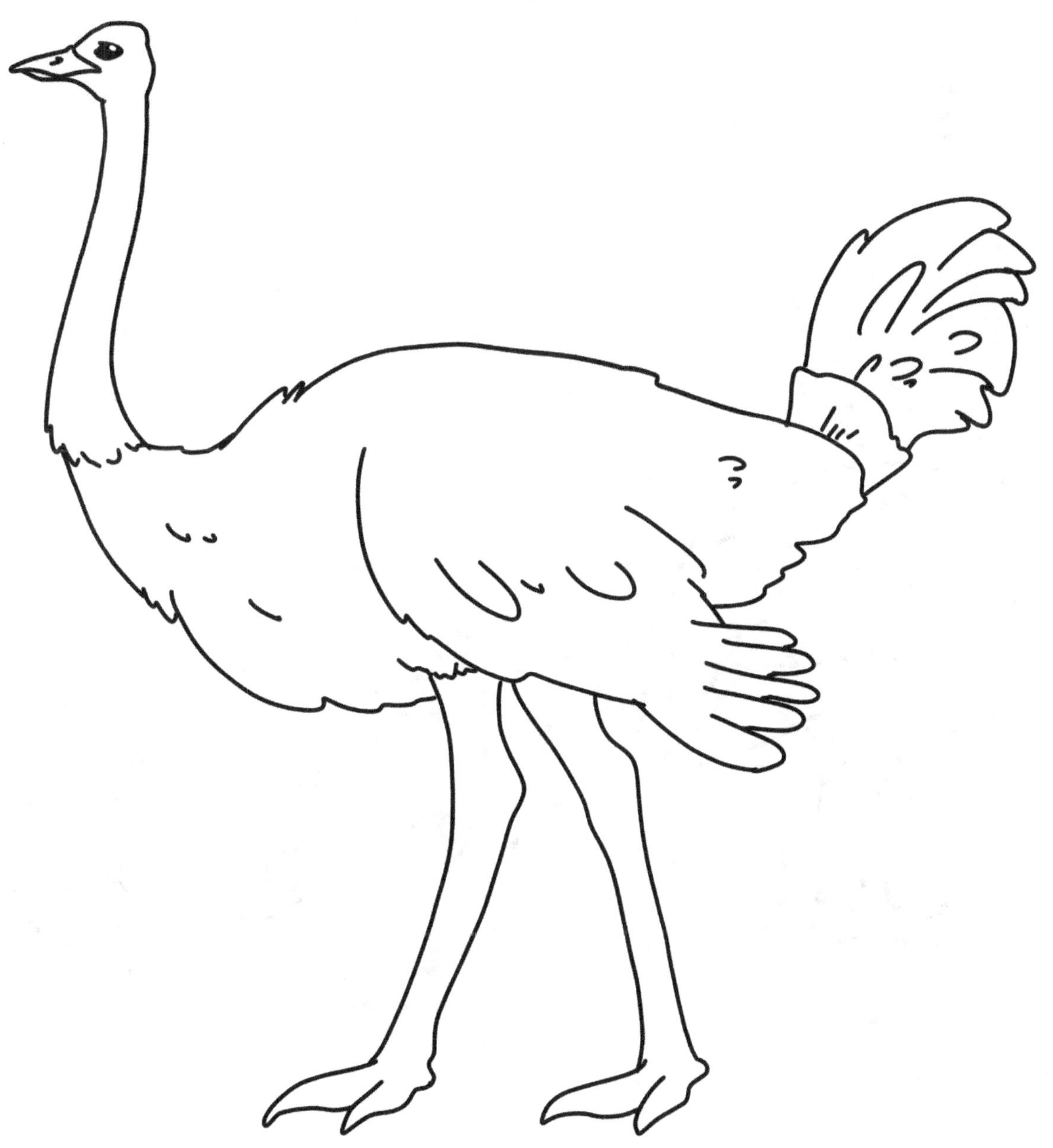

Ostrich is the biggest bird in the world.
It can be as massive as 2.7 meters tall and can weigh about 159kg.
It has a long, bare neck.

Peacock

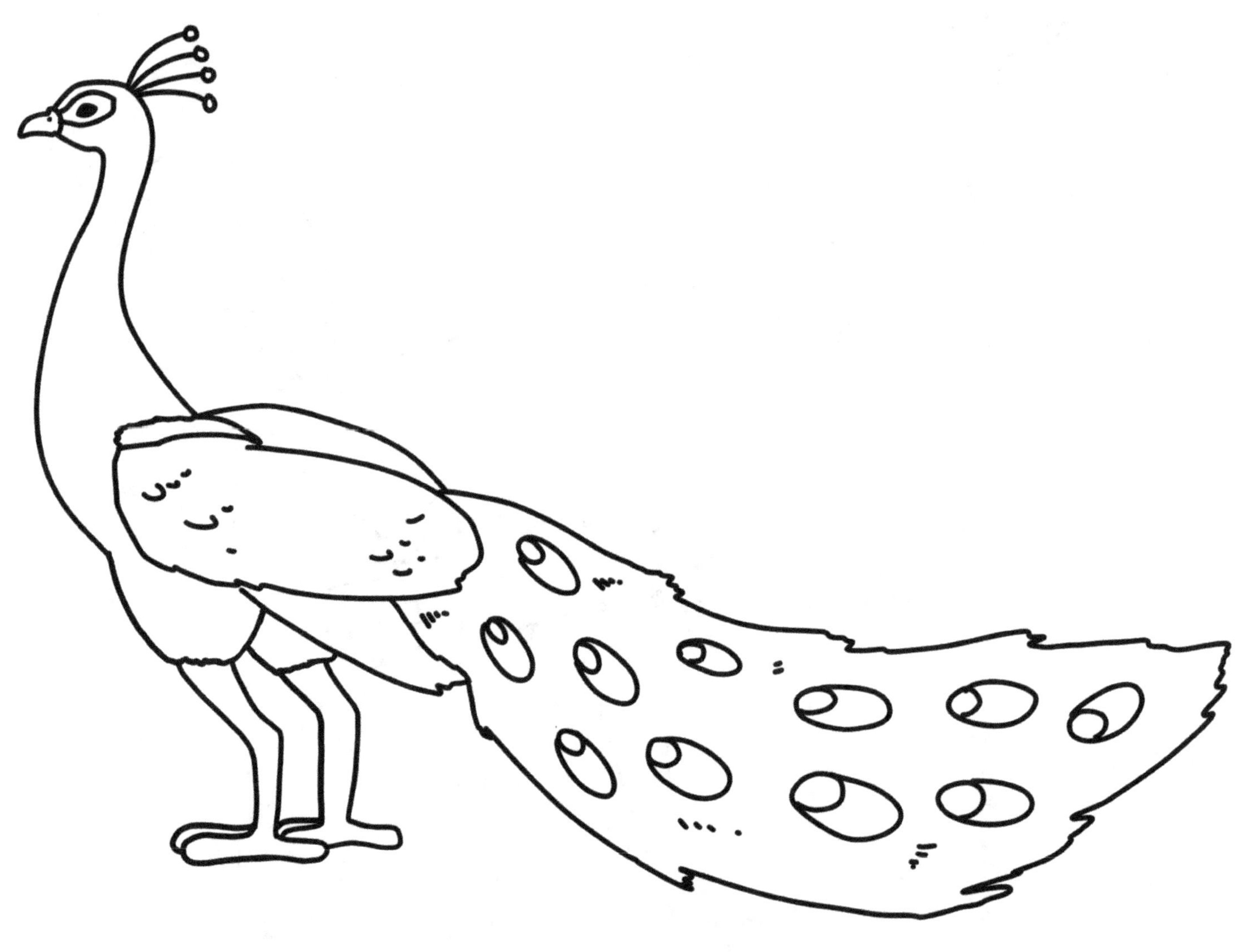

Peacocks are male pheasants that are famous
for their beautiful, long, coloured feathers.
They can spread open their feathers like a fan.

Parrot

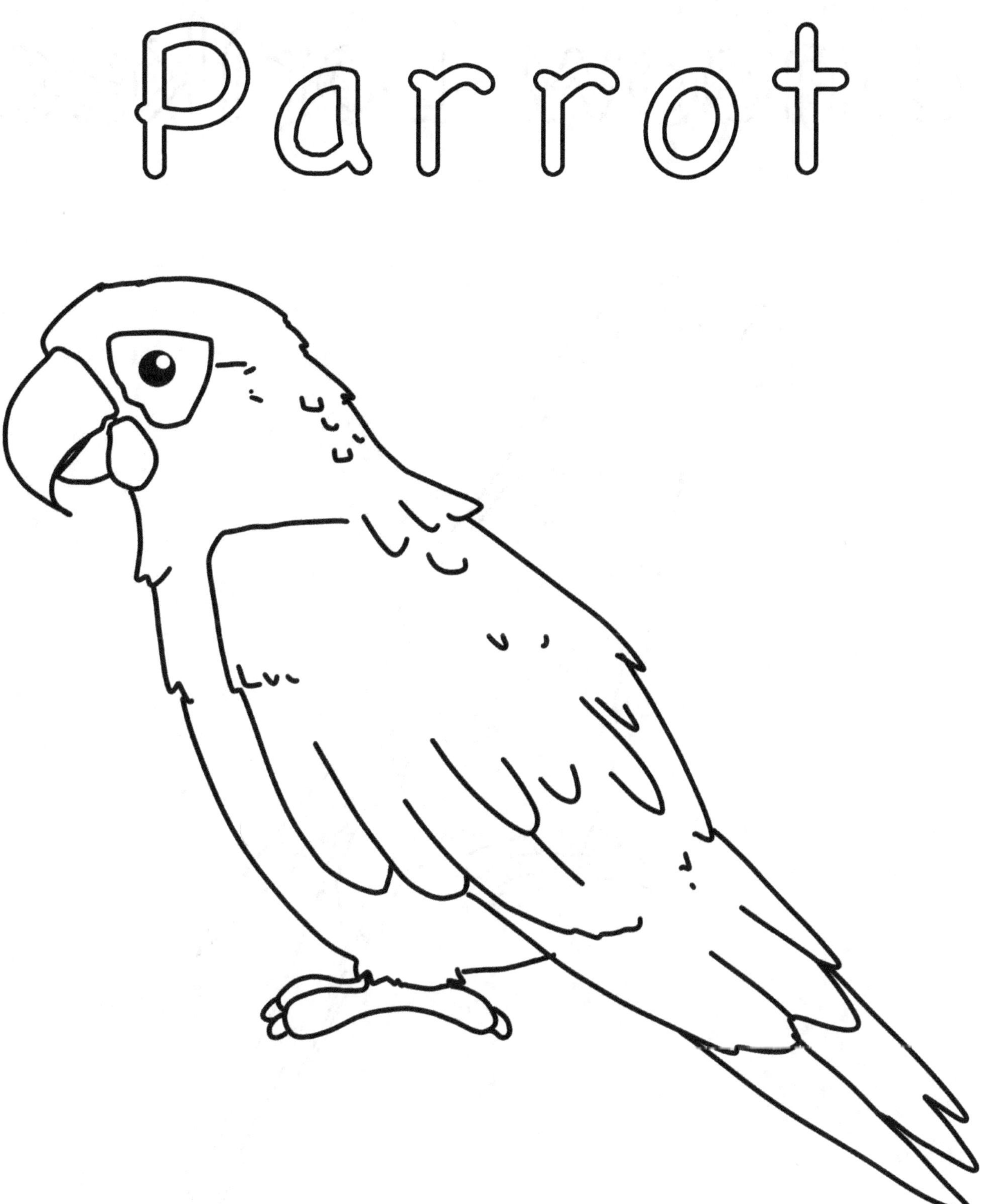

Parrots can be recognized by their curved beaks and strong feet. They are usually brightly coloured. They are the most intelligent bird species.

Rainbow Lorikeet

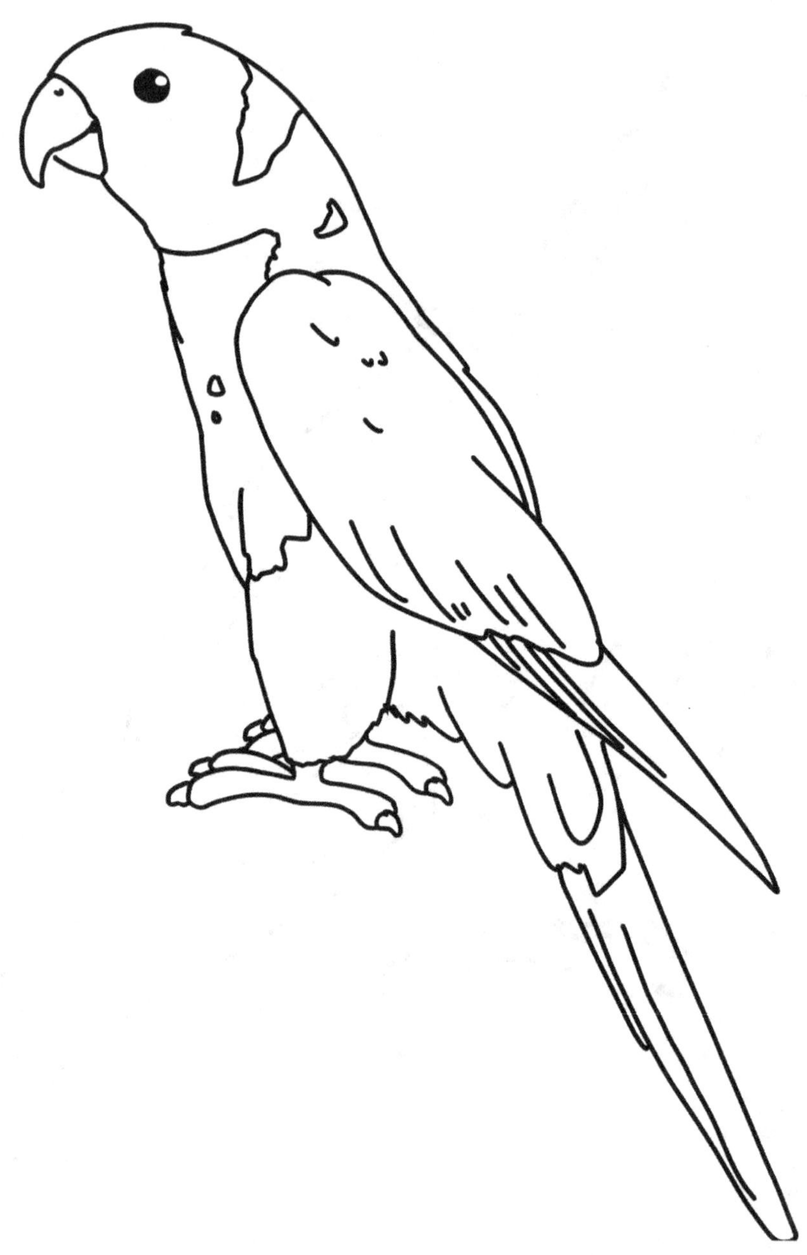

Rainbow lorikeets have bright-red beaks.
They have bright green back, wings and tail.
Their chest is orangish-yellow in colour.

Swan

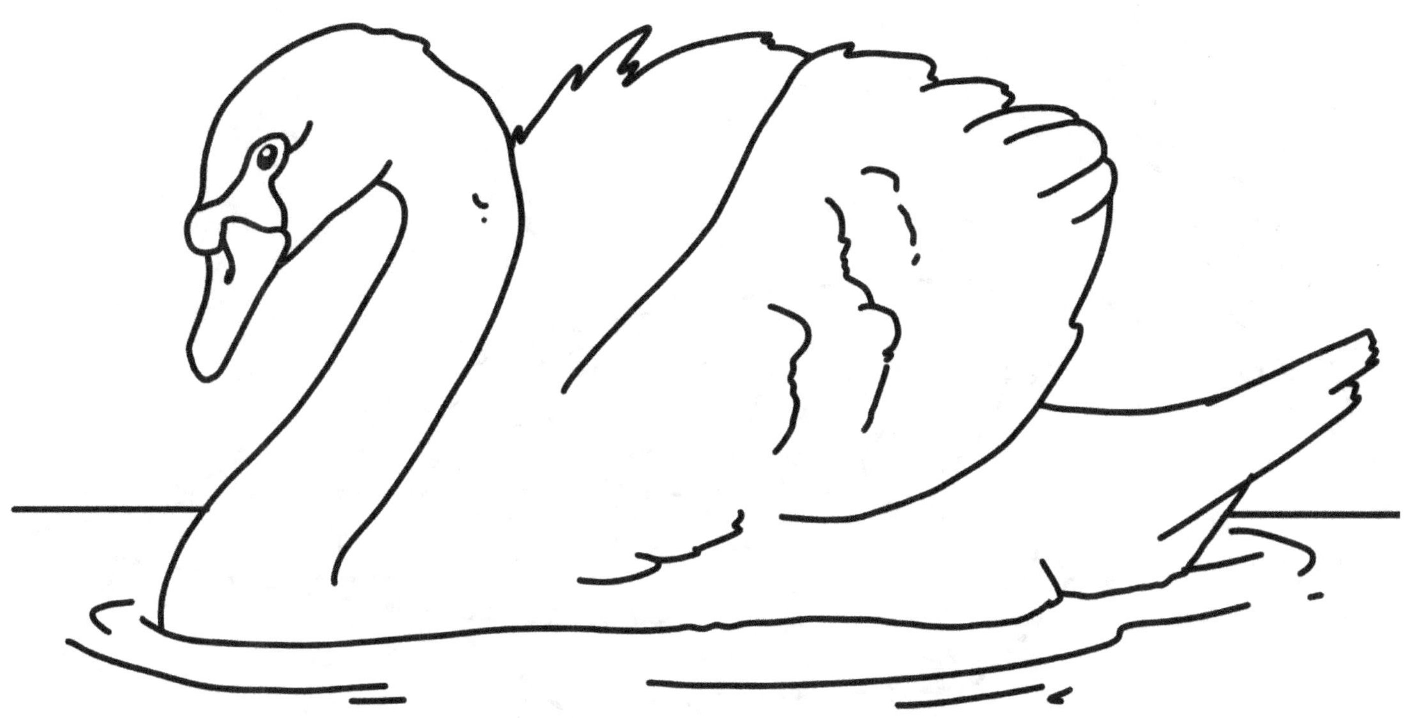

Swans are water birds. They have long necks and heavy bodies.
They swim so gracefully that it seems they're
just gliding across the water.

Wood Pecker

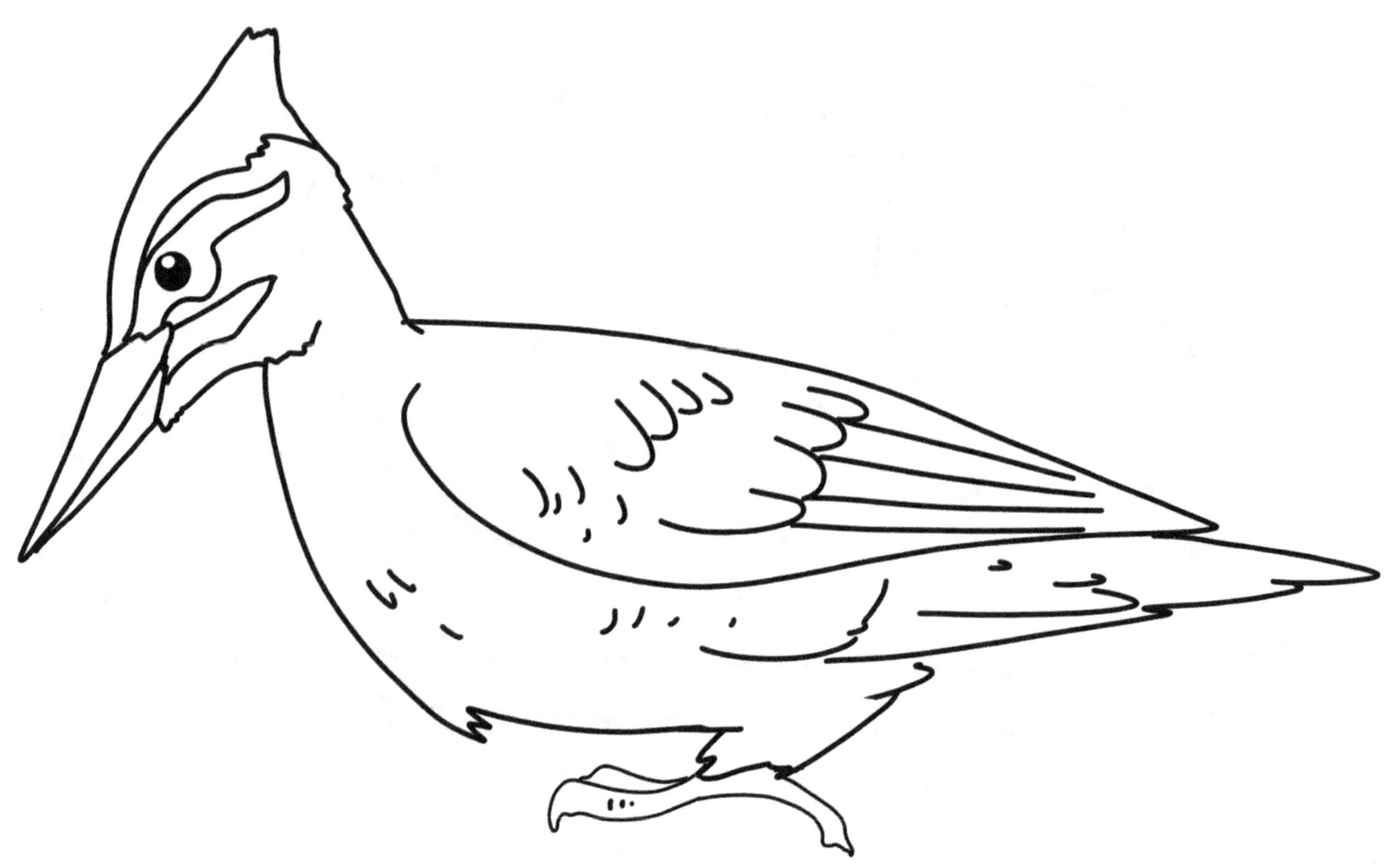

Woodpeckers are small birds that have powerful beaks. They can hammer into the trees with their beaks and hunt for small insects inside them.

Wood Pigeon

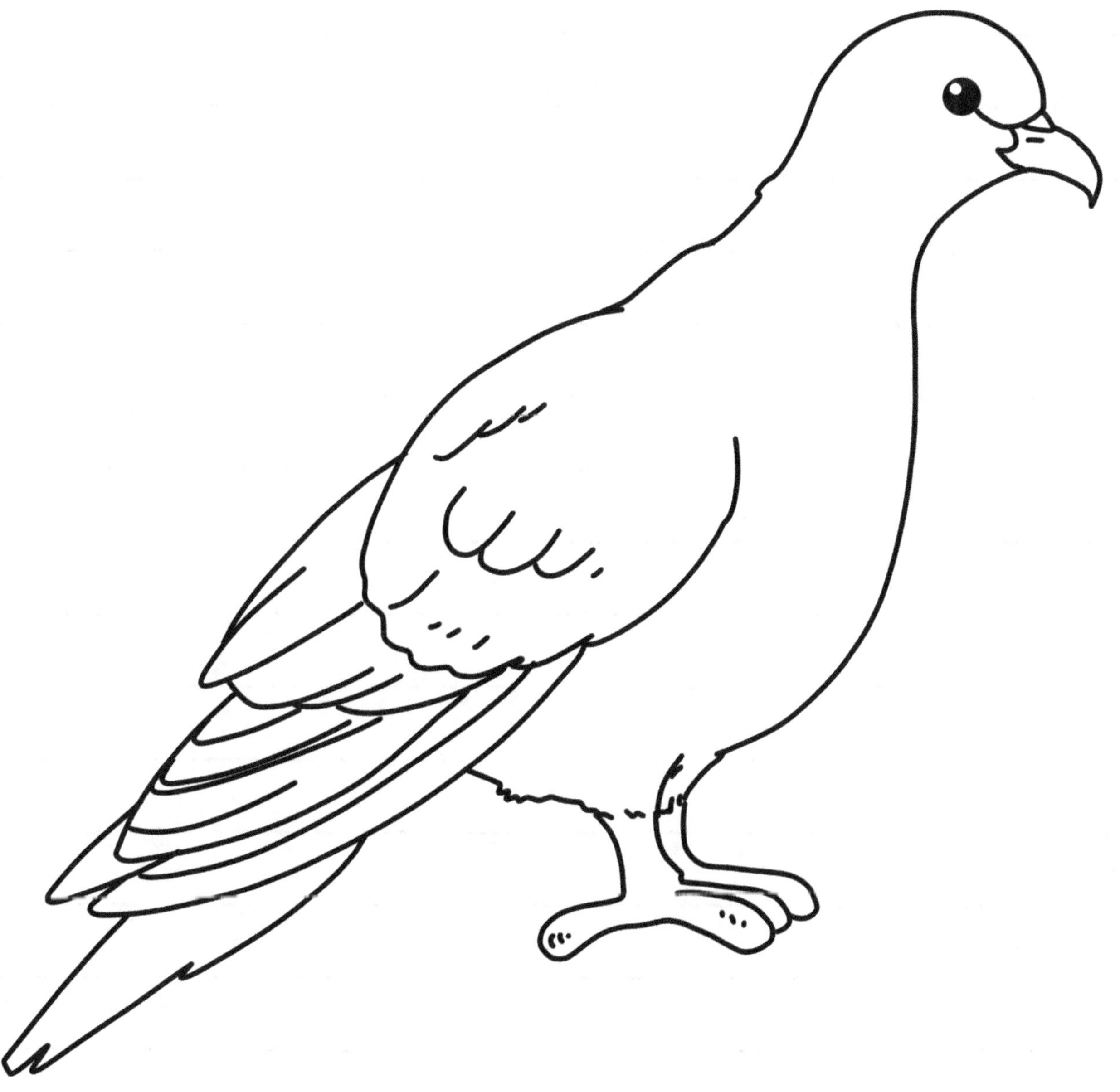

This is a giant pigeon. It takes food from the bird table. These are large dumpy-looking birds that parade around the garden, usually in pairs.

Name your favorite bird and write a few lines about it

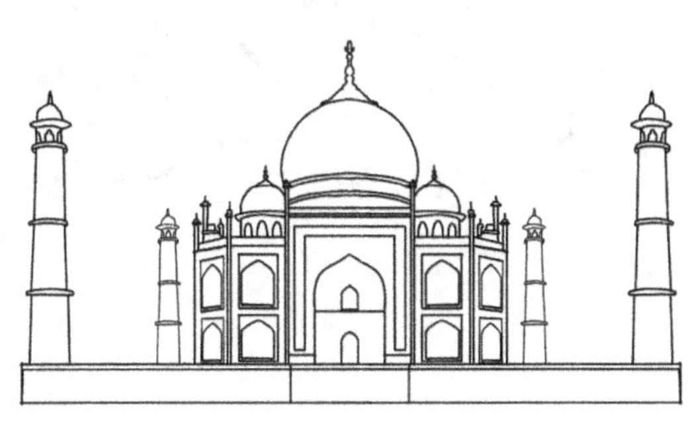

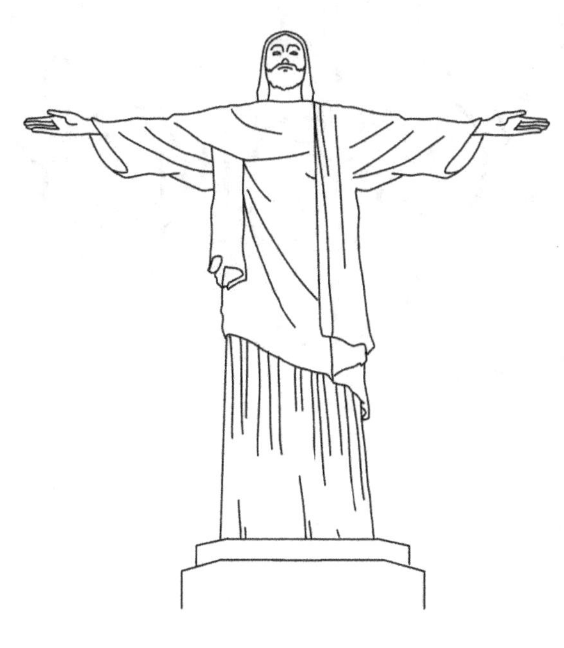

MONUMENTS

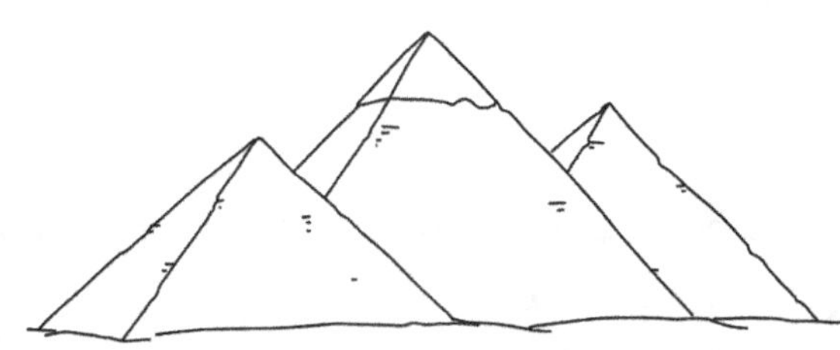

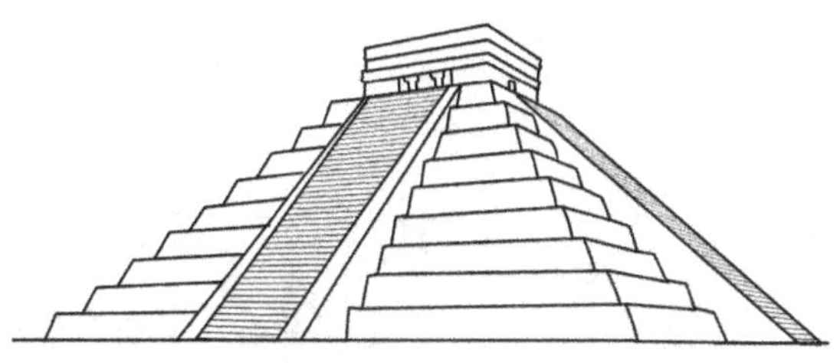

Chichen Itza

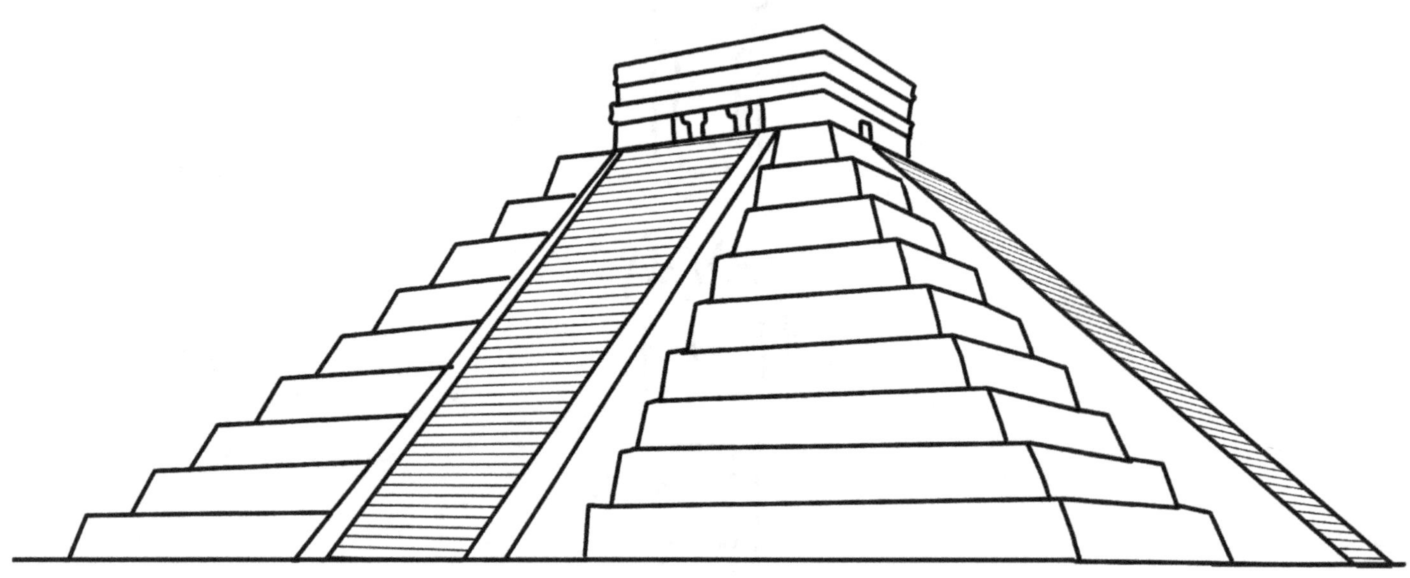

Chichen Itza has stepped pyramids, columned
arcades, temples and other stone structures.
These were all sacred to the Maya.

Christ The Redeemer

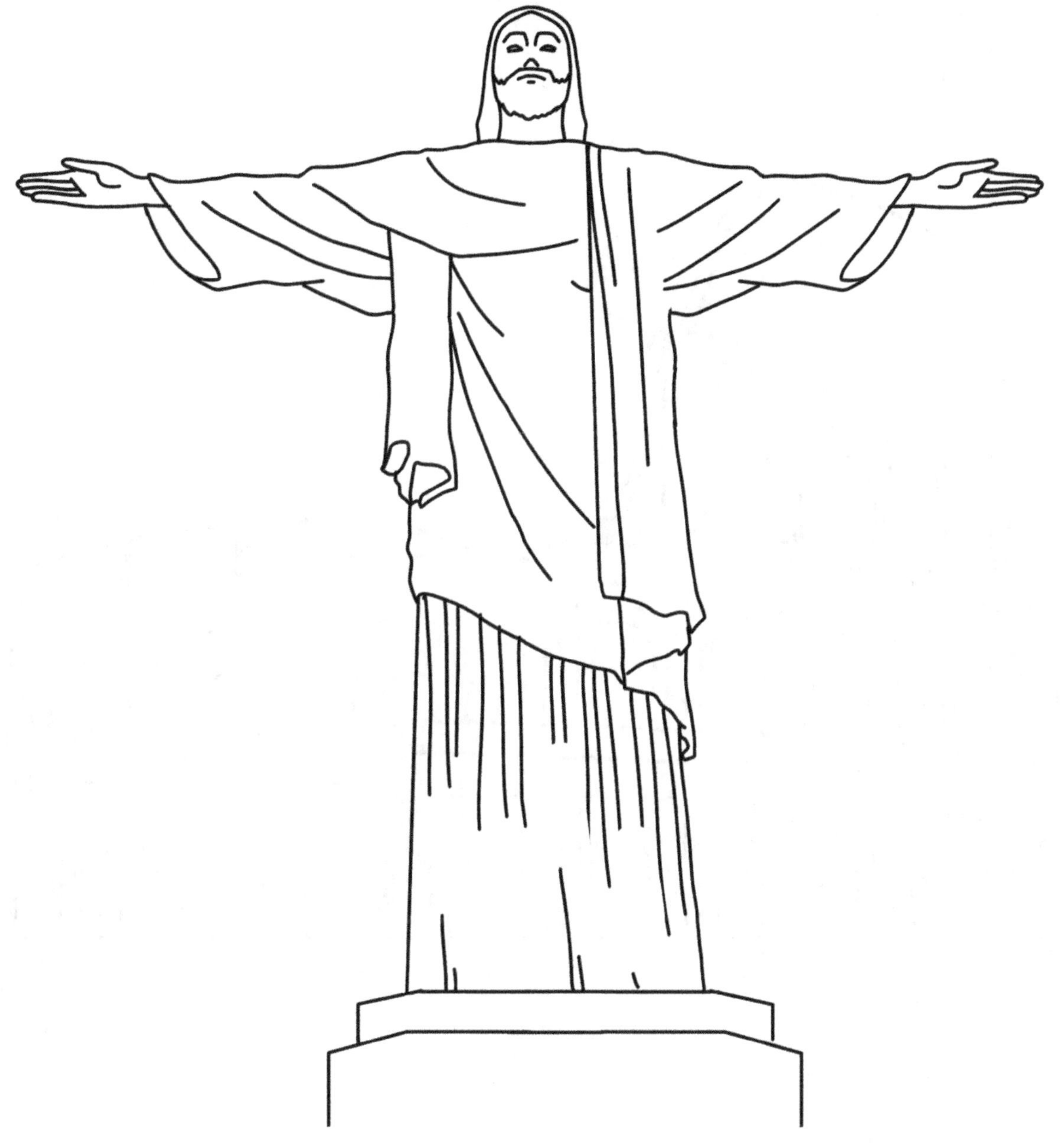

Situated in Rio de Janeiro, Brazil,
Christ the Redeemer's statue is symbolic protector of people.
It protects the urban environment.

Colosseum

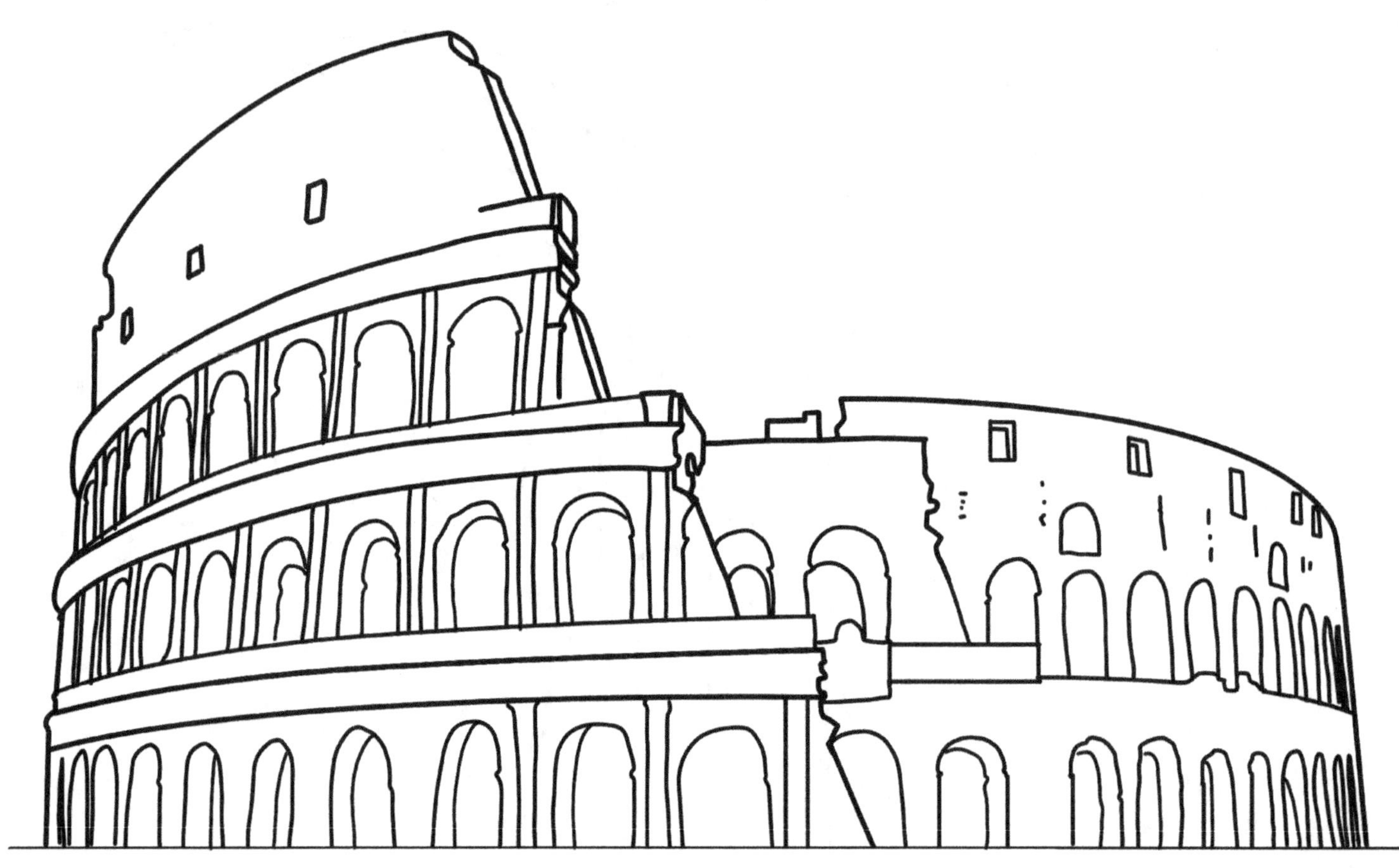

Colosseum is an oval-shaped amphitheatre in Rome.
It hosted events like gladiatorial games.
It was built in the reign of Flavian emperors.

Greatwall Of China

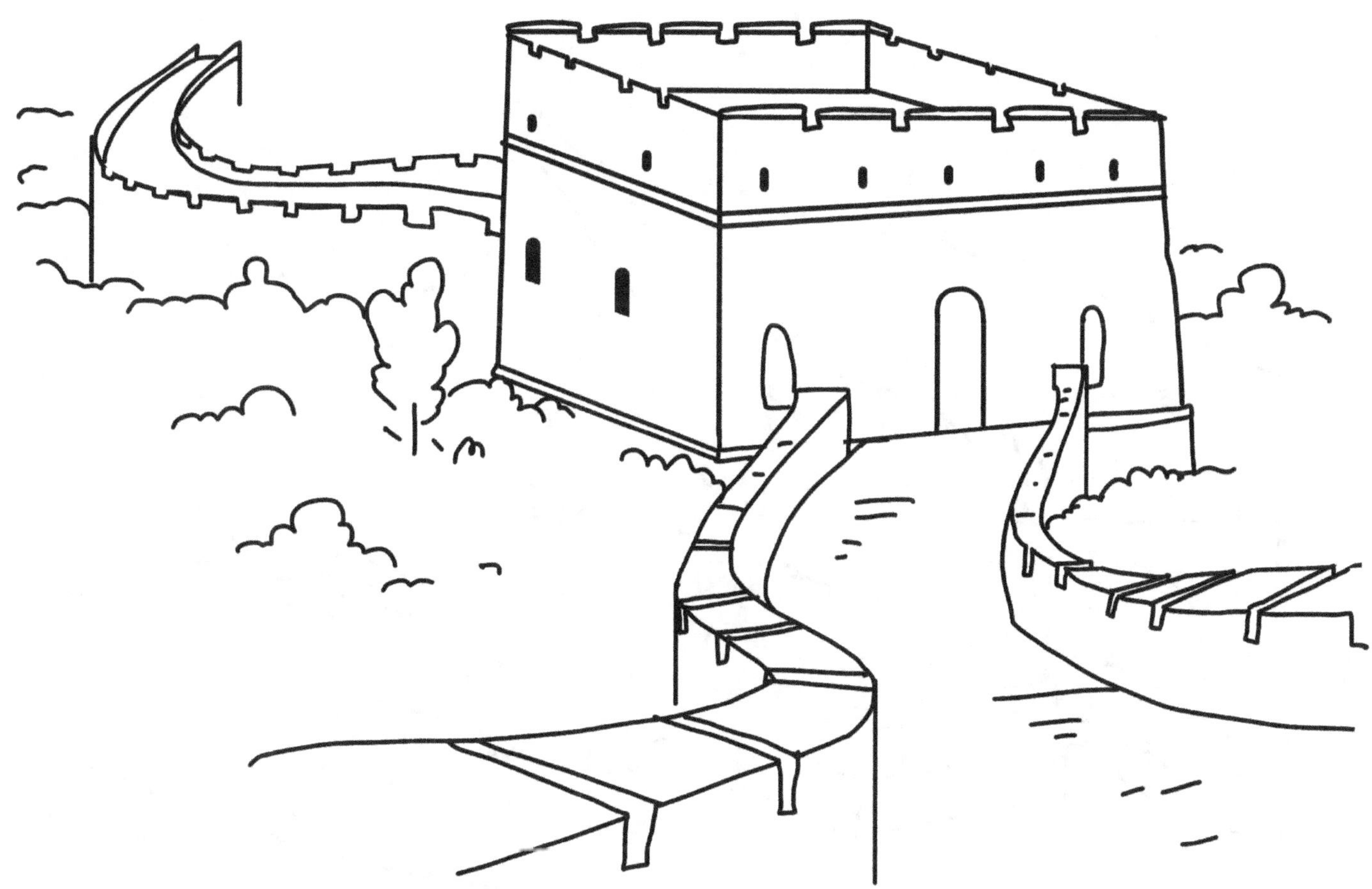

The Great Wall of China is the biggest wall in the world.
It is an ancient wall made of cement, bricks,
rocks and powdered dirt.

Machu Picchu

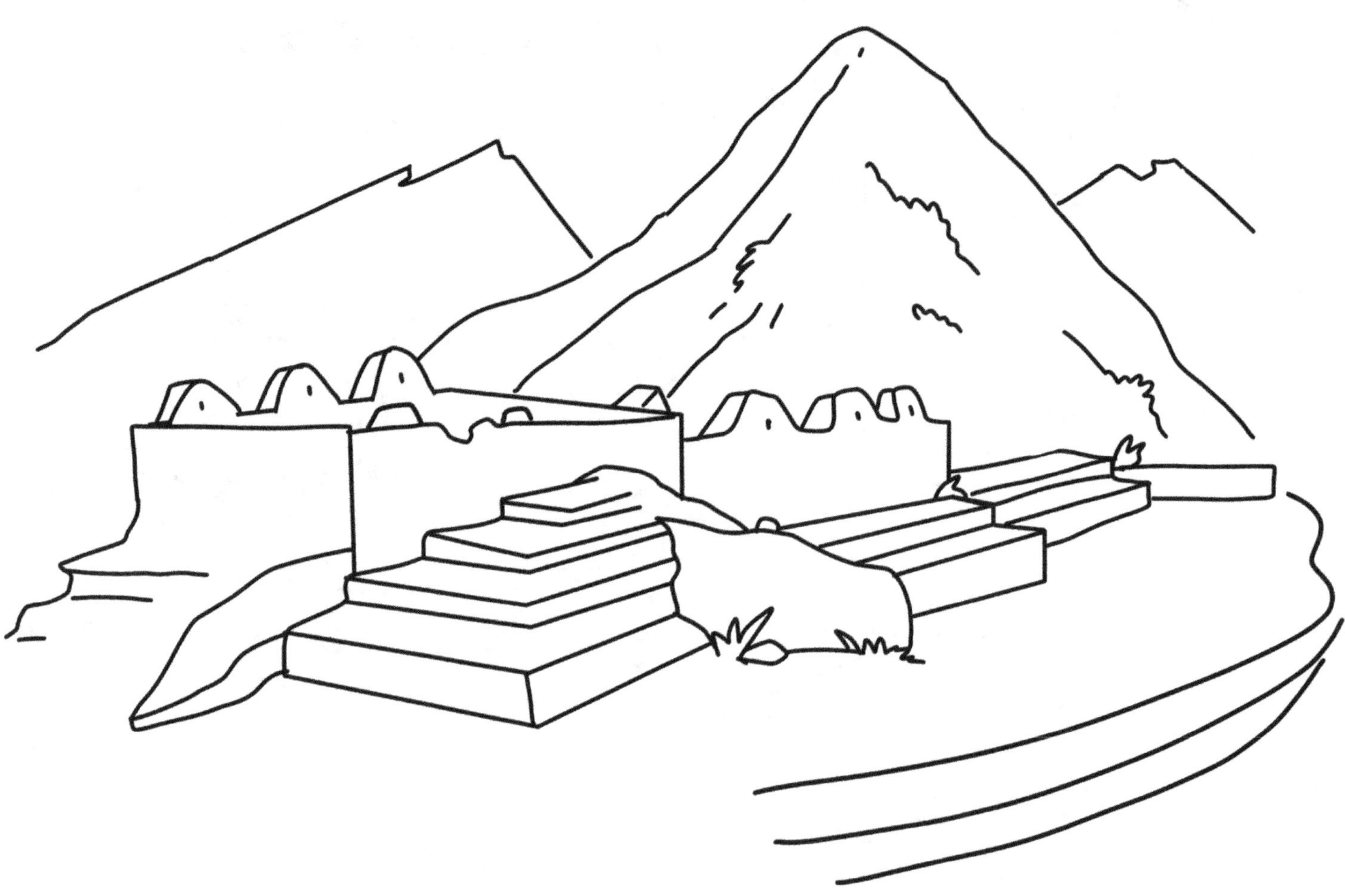

Machu Picchu is a pre-Columbian site in Peru, S. America. The Incas built it in the 15th century on a mountain ridge.

Petra

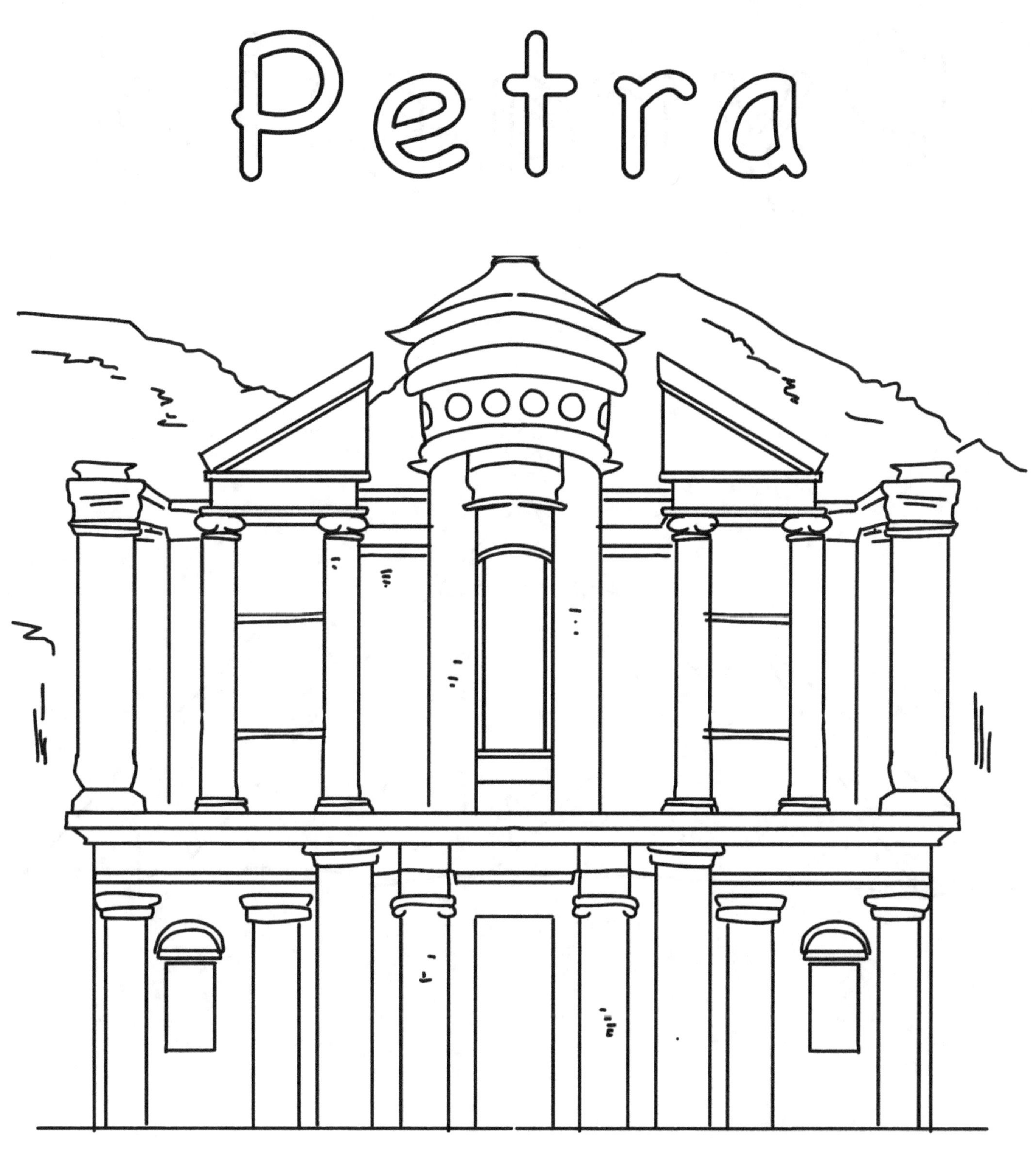

Petra is a fascinating ancient city. It is among the
most famous historic archaeological sites.
It is a world heritage site.

Pyramid

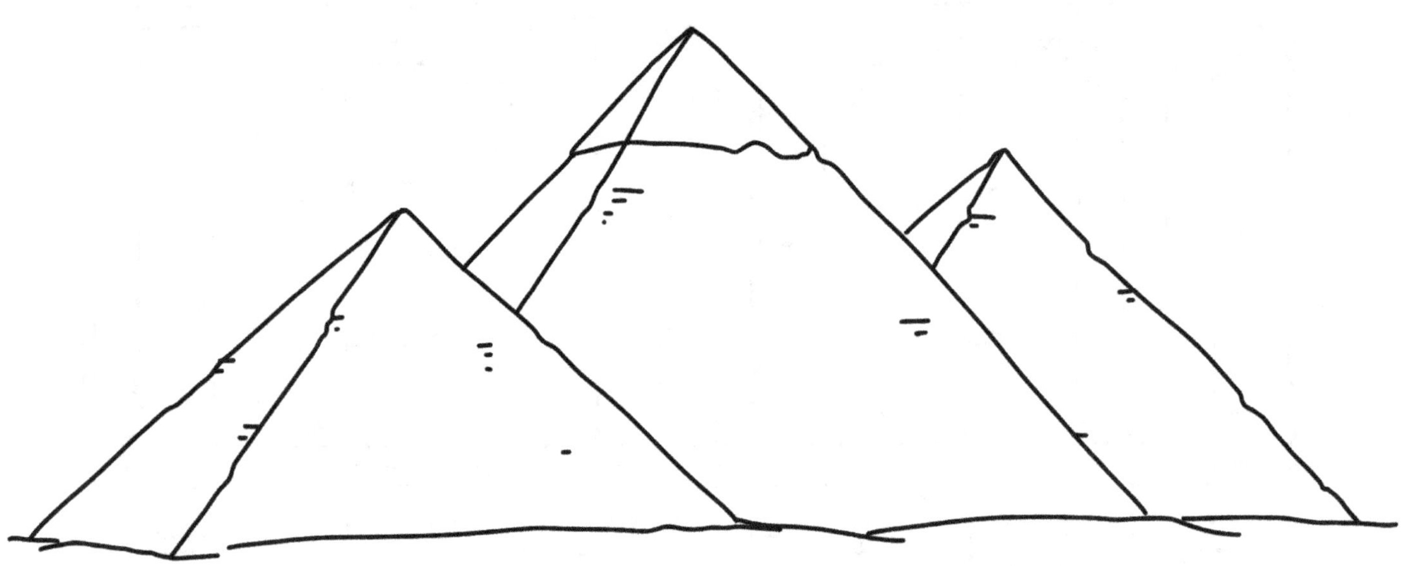

A pyramid is a vast structure that has four sides. It slopes upwards and meets at one point. The base of the pyramid is rectangular, and the sides are triangle.

Taj Mahal

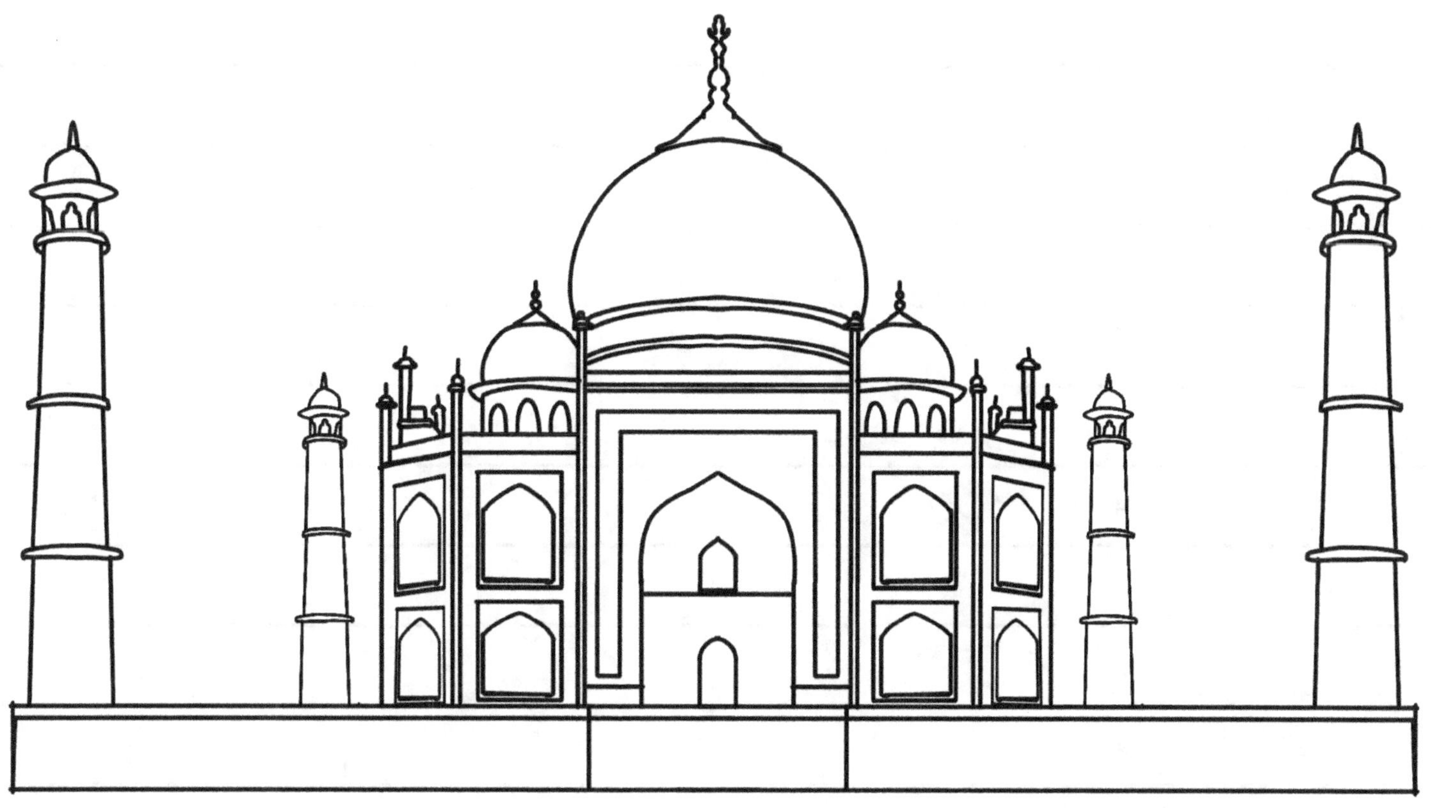

Taj Mahal is among the most beautiful monuments in the world. It is located in Agra, India. Ruler Shah Jahan got Taj Mahal built in the memory of his wife, Mumtaz Mahal.

Name your favorite monument or the worlds of wonder and write a few lines about it